Series/Number 07-098

RANDOM FACTORS IN ANOVA

SALLY JACKSON
University of Arizona

DALE E. BRASHERS
The Ohio State University

SAGE PUBLICATIONS
International Educational and Professional Publisher
Thousand Oaks   London   New Delhi

For information address:

 SAGE Publications, Inc.
2455 Teller Road
Thousand Oaks, California 91320

SAGE Publications Ltd.
6 Bonhill Street
London EC2A 4PU
United Kingdom

SAGE Publications India Pvt. Ltd.
M-32 Market
Greater Kailash I
New Delhi 110 048 India

Printed in the United States of America

Library of Congress Catalog Card No. 89-043409

Jackson, Sally Ann, 1952-
     Random factors in ANOVA / Sally Jackson, Dale E. Brashers.
          p.   cm.—(Quantitative applications in the social sciences; 98)
     Includes bibliographical references.
     ISBN 0-8039-5090-X (pb)
     1. Social sciences—Statistical methods.   2. Analysis of variance.
     I. Brashers, Dale E.   II. Title.   III. Series: Sage university
     papers series. Quantitative applications in the social sciences; no. 98.
     HA31.35.J33   1994
     300′.1′519538—dc20   93-36726

94   95   96   97   98   10   9   8   7   6   5   4   3   2   1

Sage Production Editor: Astrid Virding

When citing a university paper, please use the proper form. Remember to cite the current Sage University Paper series title and include the paper number. One of the following formats can be adapted (depending on the style manual used):

(1) JACKSON, SALLY, and BRASHERS, DALE E. (1994) Random Factors in ANOVA. Sage University Paper series on Quantitative Applications in the Social Sciences, 07-098. Thousand Oaks, CA: Sage.

OR

(2) Jackson, S., & Brashers, D. E. (1994). *Random factors in ANOVA* (Sage University Paper series on Quantitative Applications in the Social Sciences, series no. 07-098). Thousand Oaks, CA: Sage.

CONTENTS

SERIES EDITOR'S INTRODUCTION

With the analysis of variance (ANOVA), the usual assumption is that factors are fixed. That is, the selected levels of an independent variable pose a theoretically meaningful, if not exhaustive, contrast. However, factors in ANOVA may also be random. That is, the levels of an independent variable may be but a sample of possible values, not carrying in themselves much meaning. While random factors in ANOVA is a known problem in the statistical literature, it has received little practical exposition. The volume in hand fills that gap, carefully laying out the difficulties and solutions surrounding this controversial topic.

Professors Jackson and Brashers explicate the material by working through several well-chosen examples, including the assessment of the effects of managerial style, teaching methods, advertising types, candidate political credentials, and experimental confederates. To illustrate the fixed versus random effects controversy, look at their teaching methods example. The research question is whether computer-based first-grade mathematics instruction is more effective than conventional instruction. By the fixed factor assumption, a simple ANOVA might be run, comparing math scores from the two levels of treatment: one classroom taught by Teacher X using computers, another taught by Teacher Z using the conventional method. One difficulty with this analysis is that resulting score differences across the classrooms might be the product of particular teacher differences, rather than real differences in the instructional method. For instance, Teacher X might be a dynamo capable of motivating students with almost any method, while Teacher Z might be uniformly lackluster. To overcome such a confound, the teachers in the experiment could be drawn from a larger pool of qualified teachers, then randomly assigned to employ one instructional method or the other. The teachers finally chosen, then, are considered as a random factor. In general, random factors are brought into experimental designs to reduce threats to validity.

When a random factor is mistakenly treated as fixed, the statistical consequences can be serious. In particular, Type I error (the null hypothesis is rejected when it should not be) is more likely. The authors discuss how to incorporate random factors into an experimental design with other factors, focusing especially on *nesting* and *crossing*. The simplest design—one fixed factor crossed with one random factor—is referred to as a *mixed factorial*. Once a random factor is incorporated, the statistical testing becomes more complicated, in a manner similar to that for ANOVA with repeated measures (on the latter, see the Girden monograph, No. 84, this series). The essential differences stem from the fact that the error term now contains additional variance, because the levels of the random variable are a sample, not exhaustive.

Jackson and Brashers observe that random factors in ANOVA are little used, but highly useful. This volume should spread their use for a couple of reasons. First, the nature and consequences of the problem are lucidly presented. Second, the computer programs necessary for these more complicated designs are treated in detail. Discussion of how to adapt two leading packages—SAS and SPSSX—for analysis of designs with random factors has special value. Careful application of these designs should yield clear validity gains in a wide variety of experimental settings.

—*Michael S. Lewis-Beck*
Series Editor

PREFACE

This volume treats an advanced topic in ANOVA and hence presumes familiarity with ANOVA fundamentals as presented, for example, by Iverson and Norpoth (1987). Notation used is similar to that used by Iverson and Norpoth and by Girden (1992): Capital letters (A, B, C) are used to name explanatory factors in a design and lowercase y with appropriate subscripts is used to represent the dependent measure. To represent means for levels of a factor, a simplified notation is used when not ambiguous: $\bar{y}$ is the overall mean for all scores, $\bar{y}_i$ is the mean score for the ith level of the factor whose levels are indexed with i, $\bar{y}_j$ is the mean score for the jth level of the factor whose levels are indexed with j, and so on. When necessary (e.g., to reference one particular level of one particular factor), the notation may include a dot $\cdot$ in place of a subscript letter to indicate averaging across all the levels of a factor.

Thanks are due to several people who helped us to develop this volume into its present form. Darrell Sabers and Linda Molm offered many helpful suggestions during the planning phase. Pete Jorgensen and Tom Reichert tested the method for generating expected mean squares. The scope of the project was broadened and the content greatly enriched by the suggestions of Professor Michael Lewis-Beck and several anonymous readers.

RANDOM FACTORS IN ANOVA

SALLY JACKSON
University of Arizona

DALE E. BRASHERS
The Ohio State University

1. FIXED AND RANDOM FACTORS

In the analysis of variance, a distinction is made between fixed and random factors. This distinction turns on the nature of the factor's levels. A fixed factor is one whose levels are chosen to represent the precise contrast (or set of contrasts) of interest in the research. Theoretically important classifications or experimentally manipulated variables (what we normally think of as explanatory variables) are usually treated as fixed, as are variables for which the levels actually studied are an exhaustive set of all possible levels. For example, in a study comparing males and females on some attribute the variable "gender" would be treated as a fixed effect, because the contrast exhausts the possible levels of the variable (male and female).

A *random* factor is one whose levels are drawn from some larger pool of equally usable levels, often as a sample of interchangeable conditions or as the context for a treatment. Unlike the levels of fixed factors, the levels of random factors do not represent specific interesting conditions. More often, they are arbitrary samples from large sets of other equally acceptable levels.

A natural question is why a researcher would ever choose arbitrary levels of a factor—because the levels themselves are not of interest. In exploring the answer to this question, it may be helpful to keep in mind the most common of random factors in social and behavioral research: subjects (e.g., human respondents). Common ways of describing experimental designs may lead us to overlook the subjects factor or to think that subjects have some special status that is not best captured by the idea of "a factor." For example, a design with one *explanatory* factor is often described as a "one factor design," a design with two *explanatory* factors as a "two factor design," a design in which the explanatory factor

1

is crossed with the subjects factor as a "one factor repeated measures design," and so on. Although we do not commonly speak of a "subject factor," to speak of a subject factor is both useful and correct.

Anyone who has had any experience with the analysis of variance has had some experience in dealing with random factors, at least for the special case of subjects. This is important, because it provides a basis for analogical reasoning about designs in which other random factors occur. Our specific concern is for designs in which there are random factors other than subjects, usually in addition to subjects.

When and why are random factors other than subjects used? Most commonly, random factors are incorporated into experiments for one of three purposes: to measure variability associated with some condition, to avoid confounds that are otherwise difficult or impossible to control, and to improve generalizability.

Some preliminary examples will help to clarify the fixed/random distinction and to illustrate the varied roles random factors can play in research.

Example 1. A behavioral researcher has devised a method for evaluating "managerial style" by observing the ordinary workday interactions of managers and rating certain kinds of occurrences. Because the evaluation method is to be applied in the field by many different evaluators, it is important to find out whether ratings vary much or little from one trained evaluator to another. To explore this question, three evaluators are trained, then all three go into the field as a team to evaluate the behavior of 20 individual managers. Of interest is how much variability there is from rater to rater in how a manager is evaluated. The analysis must address this interest in some fashion, for example, by examining differences in evaluation from rater to rater. In a design of this kind, the individual raters are just a sample of possible raters (on a par with the managers who serve as subjects), and hence can be considered levels of a random factor. This is a very typical problem in the design of measurement procedures, a type of problem that has given rise to a large body of work known as "generalizability theory" (Cronbach, Gleser, Nanda, & Rajaratnam, 1972; Shavelson & Webb, 1991).

Example 2. An educational researcher is interested in whether two methods of teaching first-grade math (computer-assisted instruction and conventional instruction) differ in their effectiveness. Aided by the school district administration, the researcher arranges to implement the two methods in different classes, using the same texts and other materials, but varying the instructional format. Although it might seem that a clean comparison could be made by studying one class using each method, such a comparison would be plagued by many uncontrolled differences between teacher and teacher or between class and class. To avoid these problems, a number of teachers are recruited, and each participating teacher is assigned one method or the other, at random. At the end of the school year, all classes take a standardized test in math achievement. Of interest is whether the achievement scores differ from one instructional format to the other, and if so, which format leads to higher average scores. Teaching method is an explanatory factor, with two levels: computer-assisted instruction and conventional instruction. The specific teachers assigned to implement each method are best considered a sample from a universe of acceptable teachers of each method, and hence are regarded as a random factor. The observational unit might be either teachers (in which case data are collected as average test scores for each class) or students (in which case data are collected as individual students' test scores). In the latter case, students would also be considered random, because the students within a class, like the teachers within a method, represent a sample from many other equally acceptable research subjects.

Example 3. Of interest to advertisers is the relative effectiveness of "comparative" and "noncomparative" advertising. In a comparative ad, the product or service advertised is contrasted explicitly with its competitors; noncomparative ads offer no information about competing products or services. Many ads can be constructed in either form, depending on whether the product's attributes are compared to competing products ("Flash toothpaste whitens teeth better than any leading brand") or simply claimed for the advertised product ("Flash toothpaste is an excellent whitener"). The effectiveness of contrasting versions can be evaluated by presenting them to respondents who report on their attitudes toward the product or on their purchase intentions. To avoid content confounds, research on this question would likely embody such a contrast in many different ads producing what looks like a standard factorialization of ad type by product. Here specific ads are chosen only as examples, and what is of interest is overall superiority of one ad type. Ad type is an explanatory factor with fixed levels (comparative and noncomparative). The other factor, product, is considered random, because its levels (Flash toothpaste and other products) are not of specific interest, but are a sample of levels from a much larger pool.

Notice in each case that at least one factor has arbitrary levels: raters and managers in Example 1, teachers (and perhaps students) in Example 2, and products and respondents in Example 3. In the first case, interest does not center on the specific three raters any more than on the specific 20 managers, but on the generic question of whether rater matters; any three trained raters could be used to answer this question. In the second case, teacher appears as a factor, but the specific teachers occurring as levels of the factor are of no interest; the two methods could be compared using any other available teachers. And in the third case, product appears as a factor, but the effect of the treatment variable for any one product is of no more theoretical interest than is the effect of the treatment variable on any one particular respondent; the general question of whether comparative or noncomparative advertising is better could be approached by conducting the same comparison for other products and other respondents. This is in sharp contrast to the fixed explanatory factors: We cannot change the levels of the teaching method factor or the levels of the ad type factor without fundamentally changing the research question itself. For example, computer-assisted instruction and conventional instruction are not just an arbitrary sample from among many possible methods; they are the only two methods of interest, at least in the study.

These three examples offer a preliminary picture of the purposes served by random factors. Random factors are incorporated into experiments to assess variability, to avoid threats to validity related to concrete implementations of abstract treatments, and to increase generalizability of conclusions.

When Should a Factor Be Considered Random?

If the levels of the factor are chosen at random from a specifiable universe of possible levels, the factor is of course considered random. But the factor should also be considered random in many other circumstances, where random sampling is not possible. In each of the three examples considered so far, the levels of one factor are arbitrary, but by no means random. In Example 1, neither raters nor managers are selected at random from among all possible raters and managers. In Example 2, teachers are not selected at random from among all possible teachers, though they can be assigned at random to the two teaching methods. And in Example 3, neither products nor respondents are selected at random from among all possible products or all possible respondents.

In much social scientific experimentation, respondents appear as a random factor, even though they are very rarely selected at random from a specifiable population. The same will be true for many other random factors, including in the examples above raters, teachers, and products. When the levels of such factors are selected as representatives of a large class of other such cases, their selection should approximate as closely as possible a random selection, but with many such factors the very notion of random sampling is incongruous. Consider the product factor: The population of possible products is limitless, for they do not even have to be authentic. We will describe and illustrate three tests that can be applied to decide whether to treat a factor as fixed or as random.

First, it is best to treat a factor as random when its specific levels could be replaced by other equally acceptable levels without changing the research question or the conclusions to be drawn from the study—in other words, when the specific levels chosen are arbitrary or substitutable (Shavelson & Webb, 1991). Recall the experiment on alternative teaching methods. The two teaching methods are considered fixed: We cannot substitute two other teaching methods without posing a completely different question. But teachers are considered random, because any available teachers could be substituted for the teachers selected as participants in the study. (Students would ordinarily be considered random, though as will be shown later, the main substantive questions behind this design can be answered treating teacher or class as the unit of analysis.) Replaceability is one good test for whether to treat a factor as fixed or random: If it makes no difference to the experimenter which specific levels of the factor are used, it is best to consider the factor random.

In some cases, the replaceability test applies only very ambiguously. To see such a case, let us add one more feature to our experiment, a subject matter factor. We might wonder, for example, whether the difference between the two teaching methods depends on which subject is being taught. Then our design might include teaching method as one factor and subject matter as a second factor, with levels such as math, science, and language arts. Presumably, we would still want to include several teachers within each condition (i.e., several math teachers using each method, several science teachers using each method, etc.); teachers remain a random factor. But how should we treat the subject matter factor? Because there are other subject matters that could have been included in the experiment (art, social studies, health) it may seem that the subject matter factor should be considered random, by the replaceability test. But notice the difference between replacing teachers and replacing subject matters: If teachers are replaced, the experiment remains relevant as an examination of the difference between the two teaching methods for math, science, and language arts, while if subject matters are replaced, the experiment may become something different, an examination of the difference between the two teaching methods for art, social studies, and health.

In such cases, the decision about how to treat the factor depends on what sort of conclusion we want to draw. Hence, a second test to apply in deciding whether the factor is fixed or random is whether the conclusion is to be restricted to the levels examined or generalized to examined *and* unexamined levels. Consider the contrasting conclusions below:

1. "Computer-assisted instruction is better than conventional instruction."
2. "Computer-assisted instruction is better for math, science, and language arts"; or "Computer-assisted instruction is better for math and science, while conventional instruction is best for language arts."

The first conclusion suggests some sort of generalization across subject matters, a conclusion *unrestricted* by subject matter. The second conclusion (in either version) suggests a more limited generalization, a generalization beyond the classes studied but not beyond subject matters studied. It is often suggested that the decision about whether to treat a factor as fixed or random depends on whether we intend to draw conclusions restricted to the levels examined or to draw conclusions generalized across these and other levels. This criterion would suggest treating subject matter as random if aiming for a conclusion of the first type and as fixed if aiming for a conclusion of the second type. In most instances, social researchers would opt for treating a factor like subject matter as fixed.

One final way of thinking about the difference between fixed and random factors is in terms of the meaningfulness of conclusions drawn *at each level of the potentially random factor.* If a meaningful conclusion can be drawn at each level of a factor, a good case can be constructed for treating it as fixed, but if conclusions drawn for each separate level have the appearance of uninteresting, arbitrary particulars, the factor should be treated as random.

In the example above, there are two factors that might be treated as random: subject matter and teacher. The subject matter factor has specific subjects as its levels, and so long as the specific subjects define some interesting class of phenomena, a good case can be made for treating this factor as fixed. The justification for treating subject matter as a fixed factor is that we can meaningfully interpret the difference between the two teaching methods for each subject matter considered separately. That is, the difference between the two methods for teaching math is itself a meaningful and interesting question, and so is the difference between the two methods for teaching any other subject. The teacher factor has as its levels individual teachers, and conclusions about teaching method drawn separately for each teacher would fail the meaningfulness test. If we were able to evaluate the difference between the two teaching methods for each teacher considered individually, for example, by having each teacher alternate through both methods, the results would take the form of a list of which method was better for each individual teacher: Computer-assisted instruction was better for Mr. Silver; conventional instruction was better for Ms. Gold; and so forth. Although this might be of value to Mr. Silver and Ms. Gold, it would have no broader scientific significance. Notice how differently these two factors function within the experiment: Conclusions drawn about teaching method at one level of subject matter are potentially useful, meaningful findings, while conclusions drawn about teaching method at one level of the teacher factor have no general scientific interest.

The decision about whether to treat a factor as fixed or random cannot be made mechanically, but requires practiced judgment and careful reflection on research purpose. We have suggested three sorts of criteria that might be applied to determine whether to treat a factor as fixed or as random, one based on replaceability of the factor's levels, another based on the sort of generalization intended, and a third based on the scientific meaningfulness of conclusions drawn separately for each level of the factor. Even when it is not possible to sample levels of a factor at random, it is often best to treat the factor as random rather than fixed.

What Happens if Factors Are Misclassified as Fixed?

Experimental and nonexperimental designs often include factors that by these criteria should be treated as random. Many writers have argued for treating as random such factors as groups (Barcikowski, 1981), language samples (Clark, 1973; Coleman, 1964; Malgady, Amato, & Huck, 1979; Wickens & Keppel, 1983), experimental messages (Jackson, 1992; Jackson & Jacobs, 1983), experimental stimuli (Richter & Seay, 1987), confederates (Fontanelle, Phillips, & Lane, 1985), raters (Shavelson & Webb, 1991), and test items (Hopkins, 1984; Shavelson & Webb, 1991). Yet many such factors are mistakenly treated as fixed, as just like the explanatory factors in the design.

When a factor that should be treated as random is instead treated as fixed, the statistical tests performed may contain subtle errors that have dramatic consequences. This idea will be more fully developed later, but as a general preview, the effect of treating a random factor as fixed is a loss of control over Type I error in testing hypotheses of interest. The inflation of Type I error associated with treating random factors as fixed has been well documented for some design types (Forster & Dickinson, 1976; Jackson & Brashers, 1992; Santa, Miller, & Shaw, 1979; Wickens & Keppel, 1983). Generally, this inflation of the Type I error rate can be seen as a result of an unintended shift in which null hypothesis is being tested. This may yield a test that is valid for *some* hypothesis, and hence test results that are valid for *some* empirical conclusion, so it is probably less accurate to say that the misclassification of a factor leads to an invalid test statistic than to say that it often leads to test results that are irrelevant to the substantive question the researcher has posed and irrelevant as evidence for the conclusions drawn. We will illustrate this point later, after reviewing the necessary statistical background. For now, we emphasize that it is very important to draw a clear distinction between fixed and random factors, to make reasonable decisions about which factors to regard as fixed, and to respect the fixed/random distinction in statistical analysis.

2. DESIGNS WITH RANDOM FACTORS

Random factors occur in many different types of designs, often in combination with one or more fixed factors. We have already considered three examples, representing simple versions of three broad types of designs:

1. Those in which the factors of principal interest are random (as in Example 1, a study of the sensitivity of measurement to arbitrary measurement conditions);

2. Those in which a random factor occurs as a set of arbitrary cases chosen to exemplify theoretically interesting categories (as in Example 2, a comparison of teaching methods with individual teachers assigned to implement one method or the other); and

3. Those in which a random factor defines a set of arbitrary replications of a treatment contrast (as in Example 3, an evaluation of two ad types involving a number of product ads each of which is prepared in two versions to represent the two types of interest).

In this chapter, we will focus on the relationships that may hold between random factors and other factors within a design, especially fixed factors. Central to this discussion will be the distinction between "nesting" and "crossing" in experimental design (see also the discussion of "hierarchical" and "factorial" designs in Spector, 1981).

Nesting and Crossing

"Nesting" and "crossing" are the labels given to two possible relationships that may hold between the levels of one factor and the levels of another. To say that one factor is nested under another means that any given level of the nested factors appears at only one level of the nesting factor; another way of putting this is to say that a factor is nested if its levels are divided among the levels of another factor. To say that two factors are crossed means that all levels of the first factor appear in combination with all levels of the other factor; hence, the levels of the two factors are "multiplied" to produce all possible combinations of the levels of factor A and the levels of factor B. Let us review the three examples of Chapter 1, considering in each case the relationships among the factors.

Example 1 Revisited. Each of three raters evaluate each of 20 managers, the purpose being to examine the dependency of evaluation on rater. Both raters and managers are random factors, by the replaceability test. Because each rater evaluates each manager, the two factors are crossed. A variation on this design could be constructed by assigning each rater an independent sample of managers to evaluate; then managers would be nested within raters.

Example 2 Revisited. Computer-assisted instruction and conventional instruction are implemented for two different groups of teachers, and each teacher has his or her own group of students. Teaching method is a fixed factor, because its specific levels are of interest and no generalization to other teaching methods is intended. Teacher is a random factor, by the replaceability test, and teachers are nested within methods, because each teacher occurs at only one level of method within the design. Although we could regard teacher as the unit of analysis, recording an average achievement score for each class as our observation on that unit, we could also take individual students' scores as our observations, in which case we would consider students to be a random factor nested within teachers. A variation on this design would be to have each teacher alternate between the two teaching methods, using one method for the first school year in a 2-year study and the other method in the second year. Then, because observations would be matched by teacher, we would consider teacher to be crossed with method, but students would still be nested within both factors.

Example 3 Revisited. Comparative and noncomparative ads are written for each of several products, and the ads are presented to respondents for some sort of evaluation. Ad type is a fixed factor, because its specific levels are of interest and no generalization to other ad types is intended. Product is a random factor, because the specific products are not of interest and could be replaced by other arbitrarily chosen products. Ad type and product are crossed, because each product appears in the design twice, once in a comparative ad and once in a noncomparative ad. If each respondent rates a single ad, then respondent is a random factor nested within both ad type and product. In a variation on this design, we might have each respondent rate all of the ads within a given type, in which case respondents would be crossed with product but nested within type.

Example 4. Suppose we want to determine whether judgments of political candidates vary systematically with candidate gender, and further, that we are especially interested in whether bias against female candidates is more pronounced at the national level than at state and local levels. This suggests a design in which candidate gender and governmental level appear as fixed factors. And because we will compare male and female candidates at all governmental levels, these two factors are crossed with one another.

One way to proceed would be to examine actual votes cast for male and female candidates in a wide variety of races, but this confounds candidate gender with many other variables. We might get a purer indication of bias by eliciting judgments of fictional candidates about whom nothing is known besides what is presented in our experimental materials. Appropriate experimental materials would consist of fictional sets of credentials, including political platform and prior experience of the candidate. These credentials would be an arbitrary sample of possible credentials, and hence are best regarded as a random factor. Because different credentials would be needed for each governmental level (to be plausible), credentials would probably have to be nested within governmental levels. However, because any given set of credentials could be attributed alternately to a male and female candidate, it is possible for the credentials factor to be crossed with the candidate gender factor. Assuming that each set of credentials is associated once with a male name and once with a female name, the design to this point involves two fixed factors (candidate gender and governmental level) crossed with one another, and one random factor (credentials) nested within governmental level and crossed with candidate gender.

If respondents rate a single set of credentials, the respondents factor would be considered as nested under all three of the other factors.

These examples do not, of course, exhaust the possible arrangements, but they do illustrate the basic relationships that can hold among fixed and random factors within a design. Because of the nature of fixed and random factors, it will rarely be the case that one fixed factor appears as nested within another fixed factor, and still more rarely the case that a fixed factor will appear as nested within a random factor. On the other hand, random factors will often appear as nested within fixed factors.

We can imagine an indefinite number of situations that could call for other combinations of fixed and random factors, and because each of these possible arrangements might involve either independent groups of subjects or repeated measures, we must be prepared to cope analytically with considerable variety and complexity. In the following chapter, we will describe the impact of random factors on the statistical analysis and present a general method for choosing appropriate test statistics.

3. STATISTICAL ANALYSIS

Let us begin by reviewing some basic ideas in analysis of variance and introducing required notation (see Iverson & Norpoth, 1987, for a thorough introduction to these concepts). Consider a simple one-factor experiment, in which several independent groups of observations are taken at each level of the factor, which we will label A. The factor will be assumed to have a distinct levels, with s independent observations taken at each of the levels. An individual observation within such an experiment can be denoted y_{ij}, for the jth observation in the ith group.

Individual observations are assumed to contribute to the variability of the set of observations in two ways: as unique individual cases each having some configuration of individual characteristics, and as members of groups sharing something in common. Envisioning some population of possible observations with mean μ, an individual observation can be pictured as deviating from this population mean both because of its intrinsic differences from other possible observations and because of the differences of the group from other groups. This picture of the sources of variability can be represented in a "statistical model" of the individual score such as the following:

$$y_{ij} = \mu + \alpha_i + \varepsilon_{ij}$$

where α_i is the effect associated with membership in the ith group and ε_{ij} is the uniqueness associated with the jth observation in the ith group.

The variability in the set of observations can be expressed as a sum of squared differences between individual observations and the overall mean—the sum of squares:

$$SS = \sum_i \sum_j (y_{ij} - \bar{y})^2$$

This sum of squares can be partitioned into a portion representing differences from group to group ("between-group differences") and a portion representing differences from observation to observation within groups ("within-group differences"). The between-groups sum of squares reflects effects of the factor A and hence is referred to as the sum of squares for factor A or SS_A. The within-groups sum of squares reflects sources of variability *other than* A; it is sometimes referred to as the error sum of squares, though for now we will simply label it $SS_{w.g.}$ These two sums of squares are computed as follows, and it should be recalled that in a design with equal observations in each group, the between-groups sum of squares SS_A and the within-groups sum of squares $SS_{w.g.}$ sum to the total sum of squares as defined above:

$$SS_A = \sum_i \sum_j (\bar{y}_i - \bar{y})^2 = s \sum_i (\bar{y}_i - \bar{y})^2$$

$$SS_{w.g.} = \sum_i \sum_j (y_{ij} - \bar{y}_i)^2$$

A familiar significance test for the differences among the group means is the F test composed as a ratio of the between-groups and within-groups variances. Variances are obtained by dividing each of the sums of squares by its degrees of freedom—the number of different, independently variable terms in the sum (see also Iverson & Norpoth, 1987, pp. 14-15). For the between-groups sum of squares, a different terms are involved, representing the means for the a groups defined by factor A. But the number of *independently* variable terms is one fewer than the number of groups, given a fixed overall mean as a constraint, so the between-groups degrees of freedom come to $a - 1$. For the within-groups sum of squares, there are $s - 1$ independently variable terms within each of the separate groups, so if there are a groups, there are $a(s - 1)$ degrees of freedom for the within-groups variance. The variances formed by dividing sums of squares by degrees of freedom are called mean squares, and the ratio of the two mean squares is an F statistic with degrees of freedom $(a - 1)$ and $a(s - 1)$ for the numerator and denominator, respectively.

$$MS_A = SS_A/df_A$$

$$MS_{w.g.} = SS_{w.g.}/df_{w.g.}$$

$$F_{(a-1),\,a(s-1)} = MS_A/MS_{w.g.}$$

If F is sufficiently large, we conclude that the differences among the group means are "significant" and reject the hypothesis that all of the group means are equal.

Adding more factors to a design of this type does not make the analysis much more complicated, so long as the added factors are all fixed factors. In single-factor and multi-factor analysis of variance designs with independent groups, tests of significance for each effect involve comparisons of variance between or among observational conditions to variance among observations within conditions.

Consider a two-factor design with factors A and B. Between-groups differences will now include differences among all of the groups defined jointly by factor A and factor B. But this between-groups sum of squares can be further broken down into a portion contributed by differences among levels of A, a portion contributed by differences among levels of B, and a remainder referred to as A × B interaction. If A has a distinct levels, B has b distinct levels, and there are s independent observations within each of the ab groups, then sums of squares for the A effects, the B effects, the A × B effects, and the within-group differences can be written as follows:

$$SS_A = \sum_i \sum_j \sum_k (\bar{y}_i - \bar{y})^2 = bs \sum_i (\bar{y}_i - \bar{y})^2$$

$$SS_B = \sum_i \sum_j \sum_k (\bar{y}_j - \bar{y})^2 = as \sum_j (\bar{y}_j - \bar{y})^2$$

$$SS_{A \times B} = \sum_i \sum_j \sum_k [\bar{y}_{ij} - (\bar{y}_i - \bar{y}) - (\bar{y}_j - \bar{y}) - \bar{y}]^2$$

$$= s \sum_i \sum_j (\bar{y}_{ij} - \bar{y}_i - \bar{y}_j + \bar{y})^2$$

$$SS_{w.g.} = \sum_i \sum_j \sum_k (y_{ijk} - \bar{y}_{ij})^2$$

Mean squares can be computed by dividing each sum of squares by its degrees of freedom, obtained as before, except that degrees of freedom for interaction effects are computed as the product of the degrees of freedom for the interacting factors.

$$MS_A = SS_A/df_A \qquad df_A = a - 1$$

$$MS_B = SS_B/df_B \qquad df_B = b - 1$$

$$MS_{A \times B} = SS_{A \times B}/df_{A \times B} \qquad df_{A \times B} = (a - 1)(b - 1)$$

$$MS_{w.g.} = SS_{w.g.}/df_{w.g.} \qquad df_{w.g.} = ab(s - 1)$$

F ratios for all between-groups effects are composed in the same fashion as before: as a ratio of some between-groups variance (i.e., MS_A, MS_B, or $MS_{A \times B}$) and the within-groups variance. To test the differences among the levels of A, $F = MS_A/MS_{w.g.}$. To test the differences among the levels of B, $F = MS_B/MS_{w.g.}$. And to test the interaction, $F = MS_{A \times B}/MS_{w.g.}$.

Notice that whether A is the only factor or one of two fixed factors, the way we compose the *F* ratio used in testing A remains unchanged: The numerator in both cases would be the mean square for A, and the denominator in both cases would be the within-groups mean square (though the actual value of $MS_{w.g.}$ will ordinarily change if a second factor is added). But when the second factor is random instead of fixed, the composition of the test statistics *does* change. The inclusion of random factors complicates the choice of test statistics in a fashion analogous to the complications of repeated measures. Sums of squares and mean squares are computed in the same fashion as for fixed factors, but test statistics are composed quite differently.

In analysis of variance with random factors, testing of the effects of interest may involve error terms reflecting not only variance contributed by choice of subjects but also on variance contributed by sampling from among possible levels of the random variable. Recall that a factor is considered random if its levels are only a sample from many other possible levels. Designs including random factors other than subjects generally require specially tailored significance tests, to take account of additional sources of error variance. A design with one fixed factor crossed with one random factor (sometimes called a "mixed factorial") will result in an *F* test for the fixed factor in which the denominator is the two-way interaction, not the within-groups mean square: For example, if A is the fixed factor, and B is random, the test of the A effects will not be $F = MS_A/MS_{w.g.}$, but $F = MS_A/MS_{A \times B}$.

Different designs require different test statistics, so it is important to know a general method for choosing appropriate tests. One such method is to generate "expected mean squares" using some version of the Cornfield-Tukey algorithm (Cornfield & Tukey, 1956; Vaughan & Corballis, 1969), a simple variation of which is described below.

Expected Mean Squares

An "expected mean square" is the (hypothetical) average value of a variance, computed over many identically structured sets of observations.

Think of the between-groups mean square calculated within a one-factor independent groups design. This mean square is a multiple of the variance among a set of group means. What would the average value of this variance be across many identically structured experiments? The answer depends on how variation in individual observations comes about and on what is meant by "identically structured." In the independent groups case, we generally picture each observation as composed of a grand mean, incremented with a treatment (or group) effect, and incremented again with random "error," as noted earlier:

$$y_{ij} = \mu + \alpha_i + \varepsilon_{ij}$$

The means for the various groups, $\bar{y}_1.$, $\bar{y}_2.$, and so on, are used to compute the between-groups variance, but it should not be supposed that this variance reflects only the differences among the true group effects, the α's. On the contrary, the observed between-group differences reflect not only the true differences among groups, but also random variations at the level of the individual observations—random variations representing the accumulated effects of the ε's.

To get a concrete sense of what an "expected mean square" is, imagine that we conduct a very large number of identically designed experiments, compute the between-group and within-group mean squares for each experiment, and then compute the average value of these mean squares. This average value is not the "expected" value, but if we were to stretch our imaginations and compute the average over all possible experiments, the expected value would be our result. Expected value is, in other words, the hypothetical average value over all possible experiments of identical structure. For the within-group mean square, the expected value is given by the true variance among the ε's, denoted σ_ε^2. For the between-group mean square, the expected value is not the true variance among the α's, but a composite of that variance and the error variance: $s\sigma_\alpha^2 + \sigma_\varepsilon^2$, where s is the number of observations per cell. The reason for this is that the group means vary randomly from their true values as a function of the ε's, and the net effect of this is to make groups look more variable, on the average, than they really are. The idea that the observed variance among the group means is at least partly due to variance among individuals should be a familiar concept; even in the absence of true group or treatment effects, we do not expect sample group means to be identical.

An analysis of expected mean squares involves a conceptual decomposition of an observed variance into the sources that are assumed to contribute to it. In the simple case considered above, the observed variance among group means would be assumed to be a composite of true group-to-group differences and other variance due to sampling of individuals. In more complicated cases, there will be more sources of variance to worry about, but the basic idea remains the same: Any observed variance can be represented as a sum of one or more variance components.

To figure out expected mean squares "from scratch" is, in most cases, quite complicated. However, the task can be done mechanically using a set of easily applied rules, such as the following system (adapted from Keppel, 1982, and Glass & Stanley, 1970; see also Winer, 1971, for a quite different procedure built on the same principles).

Step 1: Description of the design.

a. List all of the factors in the design, including subjects, and assign a letter to each one to use as a label. Some method should be found to distinguish fixed from random factors. One convenient method is to use uppercase letters to label fixed factors and lowercase letters to label random factors.

b. If the levels of any factor are nested under levels of another factor, this should be indicated by explicitly labeling the nested factor as such. One convenient way to do this is to write the letter corresponding to the nested factor, followed by the name of the factor in which it is nested enclosed in parentheses. So if subjects are nested under treatments, we would write s(T) for the subjects factor.

c. Form all possible interactions. This can be done mechanically by forming all two-factor products, all three-factor products, and so on, eliminating any in which a letter appears both inside and outside parentheses. So, for example, in a design with factors A, B, and s(AB), we would form the products $A \times B$, $A \times s(AB)$, $B \times s(AB)$, and $A \times B \times s(AB)$. Then we would delete $A \times s(AB)$ (because A appears both inside and outside the parentheses), $B \times s(AB)$ (because B appears both inside and outside), and $A \times B \times s(AB)$ (because both A and B appear inside and outside). Interactions between nested variables are permitted; nesting factors may be grouped within a single set of parentheses for convenience. For example, if respondents are nested under Factor A and language samples under Factor B, the Respondents $\times$ Language interaction would appear as $r(A) \times l(B)$ or as $r \times l(AB)$. If both r and l are nested under A, the interaction would appear as $r(A) \times l(A)$ or $r \times l(A)$.

d. List all sources of variance, including nested effects and interactions. This list is the description of the design.

Step 2: Master list of variance terms.

a. For each *factor* listed in Step 1a, assign a letter to represent the number of levels the factor will have. This letter should be the same as the letter assigned to name the factor. If the levels of a factor are nested in some other factor, the number of levels should be understood to be the number *per level* of the other factor. For example, if subjects are nested under treatments, then s is assumed to be the number of subjects within each treatment. This step is applied only to the factors themselves, not to the interactions.

b. For each *source* listed in Step 1d, create a term to represent the true variance due to that source. For random factors, this term can be referred to as a *variance component*; it can be written as σ^2 with a subscript containing the letter(s) used to name the source. So, for example, in a design with subjects nested within treatments, the subjects factor would be designated s(T) and would have the variance component $\sigma^2_{s(T)}$.[1] For technical reasons that need not concern us here, the term we will construct for fixed factors is not a variance component; it can be written as θ^2 with a subscript containing the letter(s) used to name the source, such as θ^2_T for treatments (see Vaughan & Corballis, 1969). Interactions are considered random whenever *any* of the factors involved in the interaction are random.

c. For each term generated in Step 2b, assign a coefficient as follows: Form a product of all the letters listed in Step 2a, then *cancel* any letter named in the subscript of the term to which the coefficient is to be applied. So, for example, if the design includes factors A (with a levels), B (with b levels), and s(AB) (with s levels per cell), then the product of all the levels would be abs. To get the coefficient for the A term, a would be canceled, leaving the coefficient bs to assign to the term θ^2_A, with the final result $bs\theta^2_A$. To get the coefficient for the s(AB) term, all of the letters would be canceled, leaving a coefficient of 1. When an appropriate coefficient has been assigned to every term, the Master List of variance terms is complete.

Step 3: Selection of components for each Expected Mean Square.

a. List every source of variance, as in Step 1d.

b. For each source, select from the Master List of variance terms every term that contains in its subscript *all* of the letters used to name the source. The subscript may contain extra letters, subject to restrictions given in Step 3c.

c. From the set of variance terms generated in Step 3b, *delete* any whose subscripts contain *extra uppercase letters,* other than in parentheses. Extra lowercase letters (representing random factors) are acceptable; extra uppercase letters (representing fixed factors) are acceptable only if they

Table 3.1
Expected Mean Squares for Example 1 (differences among raters)

Step 1 Sources	Step 2a Levels	Step 2c Components	Step 3d Expected Mean Squares
raters [r]	r	$m\sigma_r^2$	$m\sigma_r^2 + \sigma_{r\times m}^2$
managers [m]	m	$r\sigma_m^2$	$r\sigma_m^2 + \sigma_{r\times m}^2$
r × m		$\sigma_{r\times m}^2$	$\sigma_{r\times m}^2$

appear in parentheses (as a nesting factor for something named outside the parentheses).

d. Form a sum of all the terms that survive Steps 3b and 3c. This sum is the *expected mean square* for the source. Each expected mean square will contain its own unique term plus one or more extra terms.

Let us consider the application of these rules to the examples we have considered so far. We will walk through the step-by-step application of the rules for Examples 1 and 2.

In Example 1, recall that the design involves two random factors, raters and managers, and that all raters evaluate all managers, producing a crossed design. Hence, the two factors will be designated r and m, and their interaction will be written r × m. This is summarized in Table 3.1 under the column heading Step 1. The raters factor has r levels, and the managers factor m levels. Because all factors are random, each will have a variance component: σ_r^2 for raters, with coefficient m; σ_m^2, with coefficient r; and $\sigma_{r\times m}^2$, with coefficient 1. The variance components, with appropriate coefficients, are listed in Table 3.1 under the column heading Step 2c. To get the expected mean square for raters, the list of components is searched for any containing r in the subscript: $m\sigma_r^2$ and $\sigma_{r\times m}^2$ both qualify, and because neither contains any extra capital letters, neither is deleted. For managers, the qualifying terms are $r\sigma_m^2$ and $\sigma_{r\times m}^2$, and again neither is deleted. For the interaction, the only component containing all of the letters used in naming the source is $\sigma_{r\times m}^2$. Sums of selected terms are shown as expected mean squares in Table 3.1 under the column heading Step 3d.

In Example 2, teaching method is a fixed factor, designated M. Teachers, a random factor nested within teaching methods, will be designated t(M), and students, also random, will be designated s(Mt).

Table 3.2
Expected Mean Squares for Example 2
(comparison of teaching methods)

Step 1 Sources	Step 2a Levels	Step 2c Components	Step 3d Expected Mean Squares
method [M]	m	$ts\theta^2_M$	$ts\theta^2_M + s\sigma^2_{t(M)} + \sigma^2_{s(Mt)}$
teachers [t(M)]	t	$s\sigma^2_{t(M)}$	$s\sigma^2_{t(M)} + \sigma^2_{s(Mt)}$
students [s(Mt)]	s	$\sigma^2_{s(Mt)}$	$\sigma^2_{s(Mt)}$

The attempt to form interactions produces only combinations in which factors appear in and out of parentheses, so only three sources appear in the final list as summarized in Table 3.2. The number of levels for the three factors are m, t, and s for methods, teachers, and students, respectively. Because method is a fixed factor, its variance term will be θ^2_M, with coefficient ts. The variance components for teachers and students will be $\sigma^2_{t(M)}$ and $\sigma^2_{s(Mt)}$, with coefficients s and 1, as summarized in Table 3.2 under column heading Step 2c. Selecting terms for the expected mean square for method, all three contain the letter M in their subscripts and none are canceled due to extra capital letters. Selecting terms for the expected mean square for teachers, $ts\theta^2_M$ is ruled out because it does not contain t in its subscript, but $\sigma^2_{s(Mt)}$ is accepted because it contains both of the letters used to name the teacher factor and no *extra* capital letters. For the students factor, only one term is accepted, because only one term contains all three letters in its subscript. The final results are shown in Table 3.2.

Mastering the method described in the rules is a matter of practice; a useful exercise would be to walk through the rules for Examples 3 and 4, checking in each case for agreement between expected mean squares generated by walk-through and expected mean squares shown in the worked examples. Summaries for Examples 3 and 4 are shown in Tables 3.3 and 3.4.

As should be apparent, much depends on whether a given factor is treated as fixed or as random. Let us consider, as before, a two-factor design with independent groups of subjects. We will examine this design twice, treating the second factor (B) as fixed in the first case and as random in the second. Computations of sums of squares and mean squares do not depend on whether factors are fixed or random, so formulas for mean squares given earlier apply to both cases. In Table 3.5, the *expected* mean squares under contrasting forms of analysis are

Table 3.3
Expected Mean Squares for Example 3
(comparative versus noncomparative advertising)

Step 1 Sources	Step 2a Levels	Step 2c Components	Step 3d Expected Mean Squares
ad type [T]	t	$pr\theta_T^2$	$pr\theta_T^2 + r\sigma_{T \times p}^2 + \sigma_{r(Tp)}^2$
product [p]	p	$tr\sigma_p^2$	$tr\sigma_p^2 + \sigma_{r(Tp)}^2$
T × p		$r\sigma_{T \times p}^2$	$r\sigma_{T \times p}^2 + \sigma_{r(Tp)}^2$
respondent [r(Tp)]	r	$\sigma_{r(Tp)}^2$	$\sigma_{r(Tp)}^2$

shown side by side. Of special importance is the comparison between the expected mean squares for the fixed factor A.

Earlier we gave brief attention to the question of what happens when the levels of a factor are in fact sampled, but treated in analysis as though they were fixed. If the levels of B have in fact been sampled, then (as shown in the right side of Table 3.5) the variance among levels of A will "contain" random variance due the choice of levels of B (along with other random variation). Treating the levels of B as though they were fixed does not change the computed value of any mean square, nor does it change the underlying sources of variation; but it does result in a quite different picture of the composition of the mean square, which is to say that it results in a different understanding of how large the true effect of A is. To understand the consequences of this, it will be necessary to go one step further, to the computation of variance estimates.

Table 3.4
Expected Mean Squares for Example 4
(effects of candidate gender at varying governmental levels)

Step 1 Sources	Step 2a Levels	Step 2c Components	Step 3d Expected Mean Squares
gender [G]	g	$lcr\theta_G^2$	$lcr\theta_G^2 + r\sigma_{G \times c(L)}^2 + \sigma_{r(GLc)}^2$
governmental level [L]	l	$gcr\theta_L^2$	$gcr\theta_L^2 + gr\sigma_{c(L)}^2 + \sigma_{r(GLc)}^2$
G × L		$cr\theta_{G \times L}^2$	$cr\theta_{G \times L}^2 + r\sigma_{G \times c(L)}^2 + \sigma_{r(GLc)}^2$
credentials [c(L)]	c	$gr\sigma_{c(L)}^2$	$gr\sigma_{c(L)}^2 + \sigma_{r(GLc)}^2$
G × c(L)		$r\sigma_{G \times c(L)}^2$	$r\sigma_{G \times c(L)}^2 + \sigma_{r(GLc)}^2$
respondent [r(GLc)]	r	$\sigma_{r(GLc)}^2$	$\sigma_{r(GLc)}^2$

22

Table 3.5
Comparison of B Fixed and B Random in Two-Factor Design

Sources	Expected Mean Squares	
	A and B fixed	A fixed, B random
A	$bs\theta_A^2 + \sigma_{s(AB)}^2$	$bs\theta_A^2 + s\sigma_{A \times b}^2 + \sigma_{s(Ab)}^2$
B	$as\theta_B^2 + \sigma_{s(AB)}^2$	$as\sigma_b^2 + \sigma_{s(Ab)}^2$
A × B	$s\theta_{A \times B}^2 + \sigma_{s(AB)}^2$	$s\sigma_{A \times b}^2 + \sigma_{s(Ab)}^2$
s(AB)	$\sigma_{s(AB)}^2$	$\sigma_{s(Ab)}^2$

Computation of Variance Estimates

Notice that some terms in the expressions for expected mean squares represent scientifically interesting quantities. In particular, if A is a treatment variable of theoretical interest, then θ_A^2 is a potential measure of the size of the treatment effect. From the expressions for expected mean squares given above, it is possible to work out estimators of at least some variance components for any given design. This is done by setting a mean square equal to its expectation and solving the set of equations for terms of interest. To estimate θ_A^2 in the two-factor design considered above, we would solve for θ_A^2, hoping to find an expression in which only "known" quantities (i.e., actual mean squares) play a part.

Assuming that B is a fixed factor, we can estimate θ_A^2 by noticing that if we subtract the expected mean square for subjects from the expected mean square for A, we can isolate the term of interest, $bs\theta_A^2$:

$$\text{EMS}_A - \text{EMS}_{s(AB)} = (bs\theta_A^2 + \sigma_{s(AB)}^2) - (\sigma_{s(AB)}^2) = bs\theta_A^2$$

This suggests that we can construct an estimator of θ_A^2 as follows:

$$\hat{\theta}_A = (\text{MS}_A - \text{MS}_{s(AB)})/bs$$

Assuming that B is a random factor, we can use the same method to find an estimator of θ_A^2, but we will not get the same result, for now we must find a term containing not one but two random sources of variance to isolate the term of interest:

$$\text{EMS}_A - \text{EMS}_{A \times b} = (bs\theta_A^2 + s\sigma_{A \times b}^2 + \sigma_{s(Ab)}^2) - (s\sigma_{A \times b}^2 + \sigma_{s(Ab)}^2) = bs\theta_A^2$$

And

$$\hat{\theta}_A = (MS_A - MS_{A \times b})/bs$$

As should be clear, the estimate of the size of the treatment effect will differ in any given data set depending on whether the levels of B are considered fixed or random. It should also be clear that if the levels of B have been sampled, so that they are in fact a source of variation in the group-to-group differences, to treat them as fixed is to risk overestimation of the true groups variance or treatments variance. In statistical terms, treating a sampled factor as though it were fixed introduces bias into the estimate of the treatment effect. Not surprisingly, this bias has consequences for significance testing, because significance testing implicitly involves estimation of the size of the effect being tested. We explore this topic in the next section.

Choice of Test Statistics

The choice of an appropriate F ratio for testing any effect within a design depends on the expected mean squares for all effects within the design. The general pattern is to try to form a ratio of two mean squares whose expectations differ only in the presence or absence of the *null hypothesis component*—the variance term corresponding to the effect to be tested. The process of finding an appropriate test statistic has much in common with the process of finding an estimator; both involve trying to isolate the component of interest.

In the examples above and in all other cases, the F ratio used to test the A effect depends on whether B is considered fixed or random. For the fixed model situation, the appropriate error term for each main effect, and for the interaction, would be the standard within-groups variance $MS_{s(AB)}$. In the second case, with B random, the appropriate error term for the main effect of A would not be $MS_{s(Ab)}$, but $MS_{A \times b}$. This difference can be seen easily, if we look at the expected mean squares for each term and then determine what is needed as our denominator to "cancel out" all but the null hypothesis component (i.e., the variance due to the effect) in the numerator. Notice that when B is a fixed effect, the expected mean square for A contains only variance due to the A effect, θ_A^2, and due to subject differences, $\sigma_{s(AB)}^2$. When B is random, the expected mean square for A contains variance due to the A effect, variance due to the interaction of A and B, and variance due to subjects. The resulting F tests would then be $F = MS_A/MS_{s(AB)}$ with df $= (a - 1)$, $ab(s - 1)$ for the fixed effects model, and $F = MS_A/MS_{A \times b}$ with df $= (a - 1)$, $(a - 1)(b - 1)$ for the "mixed" model with A fixed and B random. In the mixed model analysis, the random factor B and the respondents factor are both treated as sources of error in estimation of the treatment effect.

As was noted in our discussion of estimation of components, treating a sampled factor as though it were fixed leads to bias in the estimate of the size of the fixed effects, the treatment effects. In testing, this bias translates into inflated Type I error rates. If the levels of B are sampled, but treated as though they were fixed, the test of the overall or general effect of A will not necessarily control Type I error at the nominal alpha level for the test of the treatment effect. Hence, it is quite important to make reasonable choices about whether to treat factors as fixed or random.

To illustrate this point (and to extend an important idea mentioned earlier), we will consider a typical case in which the question arises as to whether to treat a factor as fixed or as random. Suppose we are interested in a treatment variable that must be implemented in the behavior of an experimental confederate. For example, we are interested in the effect of dominant versus submissive behavior (the treatment variable) on some interactional outcome such as judgments of "femininity." Not just anyone can be used as a confederate. The confederate must be female and capable of enacting at least two different kinds of behaviors (i.e., able to enact, on demand, either dominant or submissive behavior).

To some this suggests that even if multiple confederates are used, they should be treated as fixed. The reasoning behind this is that the confederates are not randomly chosen from all women but are chosen on purpose because they are capable of enacting the treatment contrast well, and no generalization is intended beyond the confederates actually used. Treating confederates as fixed, it is argued, results in a test that permits "statistical generalization" to the confederates actually examined, leaving open the possibility for "nonstatistical generalization" to other unexamined confederates. (Wike & Church, 1976, offer a version of this argument.)

Suppose that for our hypothetical experiment, we have available some large pool of potential confederates, of whom only 10 prove capable of enacting the required behaviors on demand. Let us say, further, that only 3 are needed for the experiment. The question is whether we may justifiably treat these 3 confederates as levels of a fixed factor, given that they now exhaust the population of trained, qualified confederates.

Treating confederates as a fixed factor in a case of this kind may *seem* reasonable, but if there is any variability in the size of the treatment effect from confederate to confederate, this analytic strategy invites inferential errors. To see why, let us imagine that within our pool of confederates, all 10 are capable of producing both dominant and submissive behaviors, but that these behaviors have somewhat different effects on interactional partners from one confederate to another. Perhaps dominance looks better on a brunette than on a blonde or on a tall woman than on a short woman. Any unpredicted individual difference in the consequences of dominance and submission becomes a source of variation in the size of the treatment effect, and if the individuals enacting the behaviors are selected arbitrarily, the apparent treatment effect will vary arbitrarily from its "true" average value. Let δ_j be the true treatment effect for one arbitrary confederate, $\bar{\delta}$ be the average of some number of true effects, and $\bar{\Delta}$ be the average treatment effect over all acceptable confederates (Hedges & Olkin, 1985, p. 191). If the δ's are not all equal to $\bar{\Delta}$, then any arbitrary sample of confederates will have an average true effect $\bar{\delta}$ that will deviate unpredictably from $\bar{\Delta}$.

This point can be dramatized very concretely in the following way. Create (imaginatively or using computer simulation) a pool of 10 idealized confederates: Alma, Beth, Cara, Dora, Edna, Fern, Gina, Hana, Inez, and Joan. Assign each one a value δ_j representing the true effect of the treatment variable for that confederate. Three confederates can be chosen from among these 10 in 120 different ways. Only if the treatment effect is the same for all 10 confederates will the "true" treatment effect $\bar{\delta}$ for any set of 3 be independent of which 3 are chosen. If there are even small variations in the size of the treatment effect from one confederate to another, the average treatment effect for any set of 3 will deviate from the average for all 10. Suppose that within the set of 10, dominant versus submissive behavior has no general effect on judged femininity, so the average treatment effect $\bar{\Delta}$ is zero. If the treatment effect varies randomly around this average of zero, some of the women will be judged more feminine when exhibiting dominance, and others will be judged more feminine when exhibiting submissiveness. But in any group of three, the average effect of dominance versus submissiveness $\bar{\delta}$ will not likely be zero.

Notice, then, that to test the difference between dominance and submissiveness with confederates treated as fixed is to test the hypothesis that one arbitrary average (from among 120 such averages) is zero. From this point of view, an analysis treating confederates as a fixed factor is not wrong: The resulting test of the treatment effects will be valid for the specific set of confederates studied. When confederates have been treated as fixed, the F ratio that results is valid as a test of the hypothesis that $\bar{\delta} = 0$.

From another point of view, analysis treating confederates as fixed *is* wrong. The problem with treating confederates as fixed is that our interest does not in fact involve the hypothesis tested in this fashion, but centers on a different hypothesis, namely that $\bar{\Delta} = 0$. Conclusions drawn about whether $\bar{\delta} = 0$ are not at all helpful in evaluating the hypothesis of interest. Hence, we might argue in this and other similar cases that although the decision to treat the factor as fixed does not result in an "incorrect" hypothesis test in any absolute sense, it does result in an analysis that is wrong for the purpose. Even to speak of this as simply offering limited generalization is still to claim too much for the worth of the result, because a nonzero mean averaging across confederates does not establish that there is a nonzero mean for *each* confederate. Rejecting the hypothesis that $\bar{\delta} = 0$ does not permit generalization even to the confederates actually examined.

What is the consequence of choosing such a test? Assuming no overall treatment effect ($\bar{\Delta} = 0$), what would we expect from a test treating confederates as fixed? With alpha set at .05, the number of Type I errors cannot be assumed to be 5%, but rather depends on how variable the treatment effect is around its true mean of zero. In a simulation of this situation with $\bar{\Delta}$ set to zero and the variance in the δ's set to .1, studies with 3 confederates and 60 respondents yielded a Type I error rate of 11%, even though the true overall treatment effect (averaged across the 10 possible confederates) was really zero. If we had drawn more observations per confederate, this alpha inflation would have been *worse*.

What if it could be established that the treatment effect is uniform from confederate to confederate? It should then be possible to make some generalized conclusion about the effect of the treatment for the confederates examined, and also to argue plausibly for generalization to other confederates (because invariance of the treatment for the confederates examined creates the presumption that the treatment is not particularly sensitive to the person enacting it). Within this design, an obvious way of evaluating uniformity is to test for Treatment × Confederate interaction. A significant treatment effect paired with a nonsignificant Treatment × Confederate interaction might appear to be good grounds for arguing generality.

Unfortunately, this analytic strategy has two serious defects. First, it makes the validity of the test for treatment effects dependent on the *power* of the interaction test. Only if power to detect the interaction is very high will this preliminary test offer good protection for the main effect test. For the size of the confederate effect and the study size in our example, power to detect the differences among confederates is very poor, somewhere in the neighborhood of .13. But a second problem with this analytic strategy is that it can be applied only if the Treatment × Confederate interaction is nonsignificant, offering nothing useful for the cases in which the interaction *is* significant. In other words, this is a promising strategy only when a convincing case can be made that there is in fact no Treatment × Confederate interaction.

The alternative is to treat confederates as a random factor. Recall that the argument against this alternative is that the confederates are not chosen in anything like a random fashion, but are chosen purposefully for their ability to enact the behaviors that represent the treatment. This seems like an unanswerable challenge to the validity of the test treating confederates as random. But two important points should be noticed. First, the fact that confederates are chosen purposefully does not mean that the specific confederates chosen are not a source of randomness in the estimate of the treatment effect. In our example, the 10 confederates who survive screening and training are each judged to be capable of enacting the required behaviors, but this does not guarantee that each confederate produces the same treatment effect. It is possible in principle (and not uncommon in practice) for $\bar{\delta}$ to deviate from $\bar{\Delta}$. Selecting any 3 from the 10, we set the value of $\bar{\delta}$, and the more variable the confederates one from another, the more variable $\bar{\delta}$ around $\bar{\Delta}$. Second, the fact that the confederates actually used may be special in their ability to enact the behaviors that represent the treatment does not mean that they are of special scientific interest. They are not a sample from any specifiable population of people, but their performances may be considered to be sample implementations of the treatment, replaceable by other qualified performances. Of interest is the average effect of the treatment within a hypothetical population of qualified performances ($\bar{\Delta}$), not the average effect of the treatment for three or four particular qualified performances ($\bar{\delta}$). The variance among the qualified performances we have

observed is the measure of our ability to generalize to qualified performances we have not observed.

A side issue to note is that choosing confederates on the basis of their
ability to enact required behaviors is a very reasonable and justifiable
step to take in conducting an experiment. Choosing confederates on the
basis of their ability to reliably produce a predicted *effect* is a design
error that renders conclusions about the treatment vulnerable to strong
rival hypotheses. Consider the sort of argument that might be raised
against our conclusions if we were to conduct pilot testing of our
procedures with all 10 confederates, selecting for the main experiment
the 3 confederates who yielded the largest treatment effects. Even if the
main experiment shows a large and consistent treatment effect, a critic
in command of all of the required information might reasonably argue
that it is not the treatment itself, but an incidental feature of these
confederates' performances that gives rise to the treatment differences
observed. In support of this contention, the critic could point out that
equally qualified performances of the behaviors associated with the
treatment produce effects opposite in direction. Choosing confederates
for ability to produce large effects when we have no idea why other
apparently qualified performances do not do so is a heavy-handed
capitalization on chance that biases the test in favor of our hypothesis,
on a par with discarding respondents who fail to perform as predicted.
Nothing we do in statistical analysis can guard against bias that has been
designed into the experiment in this fashion. Our best defense against
it is an awareness of the possibility that treatment effects may vary
randomly and a resolve not to use this fact opportunistically by sup-
pressing qualified evidence against our own hypotheses.

Quasi *F* Tests

In some designs, the choice of an *F* ratio will be a bit more complicated than in the designs considered above. For an effect of interest,
there may be no other source that can serve as an appropriate denominator, because there may be no other source that contains the right
combination of variance components. A crossing of random factors will
often give rise to this problem. In such cases, a quasi *F* ratio can be
constructed by forming sums of mean squares in numerator and denominator so as to make the two differ only in the presence or absence of the
null hypothesis component.

Table 3.6

Expected Mean Squares for Words-within-Treatments Design

Sources	Expected Mean Squares
Treatments [T]	$wr\theta_T^2 + r\sigma_{w(T)}^2 + w\sigma_{r \times T}^2 + \sigma_{r \times w(T)}^2 + \sigma_\varepsilon^2$
Words [w(T)]	$r\sigma_{w(T)}^2 + \sigma_{r \times w(T)}^2 + \sigma_\varepsilon^2$
Respondents [r]	$tw\sigma_r^2 + \sigma_{r \times w(T)}^2 + \sigma_\varepsilon^2$
$r \times T$	$w\sigma_{r \times T}^2 + \sigma_{r \times w(T)}^2 + \sigma_\varepsilon^2$
$r \times w(T)$	$\sigma_{r \times w(T)}^2 + \sigma_\varepsilon^2$

A well-known example is the sort of design considered by Clark (1973) in his exposé of the language-as-fixed-effect fallacy. Treatments (fixed) were represented by independent samples of words (random, and nested under treatments); respondents were presented with every word in each treatment condition and asked for a judgment, giving rise to a repeated measures design in which respondents were crossed with both the fixed treatment factor and the random words-within-treatments factor. The expected mean squares for this design, assuming words to be random, are shown in Table 3.6.[2]

There is no obvious denominator to use in testing the Treatments effect, because there is no source containing the four extra σ^2 terms appearing in its expected mean square. However, by combining mean squares it is possible to create a numerator and denominator that differ only in the presence or absence of θ_T^2 ; Clark (1973) proposed the following:

$$F' = (MS_T + MS_{r \times w(T)})/(MS_{r \times T} + MS_{w(T)})$$

Degrees of freedom for such tests must be approximated. A method suggested by Satterthwaite (1946) is commonly used (see, e.g., Winer, 1971). The Satterthwaite method must be applied separately to numerator and denominator. Both numerator and denominator can be seen as a (weighted) sum of mean squares, $MS_1, MS_2, \ldots, MS_k$, with weighting coefficients $c_1, c_2, \ldots, c_k$, and degrees of freedom $df_1, df_2, \ldots, df_k$. In both the numerator and denominator of the quasi F ratio above, $k = 2$ because there are just two terms in each sum, and the weighting coefficients are all 1. The degrees of freedom for a sum of mean squares can be approximated by computing the following and rounding to the nearest integer:

$$df' = \left(\sum_i c_i MS_i\right)^2 \bigg/ \left[\sum_i (c_i MS_i)^2/df_i\right]$$

For $k = 2$ and $c_1 = c_2 = 1$, this can be written as follows:

$$df' = (MS_1 + MS_2)^2/[(MS_1^2/df_1) + (MS_2^2/df_2)]$$

The weighting coefficient plays a part in more complicated situations where it may be necessary to subtract a mean square, for then some coefficients will be negative.

To illustrate this method, let us consider the computation of the approximate degrees of freedom for the numerator of the quasi F given above. The numerator is a sum of two mean squares, MS_T and $MS_{r \times w(T)}$. MS_T has df $= t - 1$, and $MS_{r \times w(T)}$ has df $= t(r-1)(w-1)$. Hence:

$$df'_{num} = (MS_T + MS_{r \times w(T)})^2/\{MS_T^2/(t-1)$$
$$+ MS_{r \times w(T)}^2/[t(r-1)(w-1)]\}.$$

Notice that when the sum has a single term, this formula yields the exact df for the one mean square in the sum:

$$df_1' = MS_1^2/(MS_1^2/df_1) = df_1$$

Quasi F tests are not without complexities. One objection sometimes raised is that they are not unique; we could construct other quasi F ratios for the same design that would give different results. Another objection is that some quasi F's can take negative values, as when a term is created by subtracting one or more mean squares from others. However, unless a study can be designed to avoid crossing random factors, there may be no alternative to quasi F, and empirical examinations of quasi F statistics suggest that they offer reasonable hypothesis tests (Forster & Dickinson, 1976; Maxwell & Bray, 1986; Santa, Miller, & Shaw, 1979).

4. STATISTICAL ASSUMPTIONS

F tests in the analysis of variance depend on assumptions made about the terms entering into the numerator and denominator of the F statistic. The assumptions are necessary in order to derive the distribution of the F statistic. This does not necessarily mean that the test is valueless if the assumptions are not met, for it is often the case that even though the assumptions are necessary to derive the distribution at a theoretical level, a close fit with the assumptions is not necessary to approximate the theoretical distribution at a practical level.

As we will see, the assumptions associated with random effects in analysis of variance can be quite complicated and difficult to evaluate. Hence, it is wise to begin by asking how these assumptions are to be taken. Do they limit the use of random effects analysis to a very special set of cases in which the assumptions are known to be satisfied? Our answer is no. The assumptions associated with any form of analysis should not be taken as conditions that must be met for the *use* of a form of analysis. They should be taken, instead, as premises in a complex argument for an empirical conclusion of some sort, sometimes entertained conditionally, and often bearing only very indirectly on the validity of that conclusion. When an assumption is violated, the test result may nevertheless offer good grounds for a conclusion about the effect of interest.

The assumptions of the random-effects model and mixed-model analysis of variance are in many ways similar to the assumptions of the fixed-model test (Iverson & Norpoth, 1987). You may recall that in a fixed model of the form

$$y_{ij} = \mu + \alpha_i + \varepsilon_{ij}$$

where μ is an overall mean in the population, α_i is the effect of the ith level of the fixed factor A, and ε_{ij} is a random error, we assume that ε_{ij}'s are normally distributed with mean 0 and common variance σ_ε^2 and that all ε_{ij}'s are unrelated both within and between experimental groups. In the analysis of variance, typically these are described as the assumptions of normality, homogeneity of variance, and independence.

The incorporation of random factors into a design alter these assumptions in subtle, yet important ways. With a random factor B, we must additionally assume that β_j is a normally distributed random effect due to the jth level of the factor B with a mean 0 and variance σ_β^2. If that random factor B is crossed with a fixed factor A, we have a mixed model and the randomness of the $\alpha\beta_{ij}$ terms must also be considered. As may be apparent by now, all sources of "random" variation (or error) in the model are assumed to be normally distributed.

A second assumption of the analysis of variance is homogeneity of variance. In a mixed factorial, this assumption becomes more complex than the assumption underlying the fixed-model analysis. Specifically, in a mixed factorial, an additional requirement is *sphericity* (Maxwell & Bray, 1986; see also Girden, 1992, for a discussion of sphericity in repeated measures designs, especially pp. 13-18, p. 39, and pp. 48-49). Sphericity is a property of the variances of differences from one level to another of the fixed factor; to satisfy the sphericity condition, the variances of the differences must be homogeneous across pairs of levels (e.g., $\sigma^2_{\bar{y}_{1j} - \bar{y}_{2j}} = \sigma^2_{\bar{y}_{2j} - \bar{y}_{3j}}$, etc.). Often evaluated in repeated measures designs and other mixed factorials is a strong version of sphericity known as *compound symmetry*. Imagine that we construct a matrix with rows and columns corresponding to the levels of the factor of interest. The entries of the matrix are variances for scores within individual levels (diagonal) or covariances for scores across pairs of levels (off-diagonal). Compound symmetry requires a variance-covariance matrix in which the diagonal elements are all equal to one another and the off-diagonal elements are all equal to one another (Maxwell & Bray, 1986). Greenhouse and Geisser (1959) provide a measure, called epsilon, of how much a variance-covariance matrix deviates from this condition. If epsilon equals one, the matrix exhibits compound symmetry (and therefore sphericity); as the matrix deviates from compound symmetry, epsilon declines to a lower limit of $1/(a - 1)$ where a is the number of levels of the factor. Hence epsilon offers a criterion that can be used in evaluating the fit of the data to this assumption.

A third assumption of the analysis of variance is that scores will be independent. According to Keppel (1991), independence "means that each observation is in no way related to any other observations in the experiment" (p. 97). Kenny and Judd (1986) note that "if two observations are independent of each other, then the conditional probability of one of them, given the other, is no different than the unconditional probability" (p. 422). In the fixed-model test, this means that all ε's are unrelated both within and between experimental groups. In the random effects and mixed models, this logic is extended to the various sources of error. In general, all sources of random variation must be independent. For example, in a design with a fixed factor A and random factor B, with respondents nested within cells defined by the crossing of A and B, the β_j's are independent, the $\alpha\beta_{ij}$'s are independent (subject to a constraint that they sum to zero across levels of A within each level of B), the ε_{ijk}'s are independent, and the β_j's, the $\alpha\beta_{ij}$'s, and the ε_{ijk}'s are independent of each other and of the α_i's.

Problems of nonindependence typically arise because sources of dependency among scores are ignored by the researcher (Kenny & Judd, 1986). Consider our Example 2, in which teaching methods are assigned to each individual teacher and thereby administered to entire school-rooms as units. If we were to measure outcomes for individual students and treat student as the unit of analysis for statistical testing, the relatedness among students within schoolrooms would threaten the independence of our observations.

Nonindependence due to some specifiable source can often be evaluated by examining the "intraclass correlation" among scores within groups, defined in terms of variance components as follows (Hays, 1981, p. 382; Winer, 1971, p. 244):

$$\rho = \sigma^2_{\text{effect}}/(\sigma^2_{\text{effect}} + \sigma^2_{\text{error}})$$

Intraclass correlation is a function of the similarity among members of groups, relative to the similarity among groups. For a study like our Example 2, with individual students (S) nested within teachers (T), the intraclass correlation for scores within teachers (i.e., within school-rooms) can be measured as follows:

$$\hat{\rho} = (MS_t - MS_{s(t)})/[MS_t + (t-1)MS_{s(t)}]$$

Where nonindependence is present, ANOVA test statistics can be very seriously biased (Jackson & Brashers, 1993; Kenny & Judd, 1986). The solution to this problem is to represent sources of nonindependence as sources of variance and to make good decisions about whether they are fixed or random effects. In Example 2, the nonindependence problem is handled by *not* analyzing the individual students' test scores as independent, but treating them as nested within the teachers factor.

Earlier we mentioned that it should not be supposed that ANOVA F tests can only be used when the assumptions have been shown to be satisfied. But because the assumptions are part of the argument for any interpretation of study outcomes, it is important to have some sense of how test statistics perform when the assumptions are violated. In principle, when assumptions of the F test are violated, the statistic cannot be assumed to have a true F distribution under the null hypothesis. For the researcher, this means that the probability of rejecting a true null hypothesis may be greater or less than the nominal alpha set for the test. Because the assumptions are also necessary to derive nonnull distributions—distributions of test statistics when the null hypothesis is false—departures from assumptions also make the problem of evaluating power much more difficult if not impossible. How much does this weaken a conclusion drawn from an F test whose assumptions are violated?

A test statistic is said to be "robust" to violations of its assumptions if its performance with violated assumptions is similar to its performance with all assumptions satisfied. For example, when the null hypothesis is true but the dependent variable is not normally distributed, we might wonder whether a test that assumes normality will control Type I error at or near the nominal alpha. Or we might wonder whether nonnormality will affect the power of the test when the null hypothesis is false. These are questions of robustness, and they are often approached through empirical analysis of the performance of test statistics applied over and over to data whose characteristics are known.

We have already noted that for one of the assumptions of the F test, violations can have serious consequences. Treating nonindependent observations as though they were independent leads to bias, and this is particularly likely to occur when a random factor is somehow "lost" in the analysis (as, for example, if all of the students in our experiment on teaching methods were treated as independent, so that the teacher factor was suppressed). Nonindependence may result either in a loss of control over Type I error or in a loss of power, depending on the design (Jackson & Brashers, 1993; Kenny & Judd, 1986). Fortunately, violations of the independence assumptions can generally be avoided through good design and analysis choices.

As to the other assumptions, a common supposition is that ANOVA F tests are not unduly affected by departures from normality and homogeneity, at least for balanced designs. Winer (1971, p. 332) suggests that F tests involving random factors may perform quite well despite departure from the theoretical assumptions underlying the tests. Empirical work appears to bear out this optimism. For example, Santa et al. (1979) have shown that the quasi F test proposed by Clark (1973) is a "very reasonable statistic" (p. 45) in the face of violations of distribution and homogeneity assumptions, and Maxwell and Bray (1986) have shown the same test to be robust to violations of sphericity.

It should be understood, however, that studies of robustness are always limited by the particular types and degrees of violations examined, and to say that a test performs adequately for one sort of violation is not to say that it performs adequately for other sorts of violations. The most general point to be taken from this discussion is that a test *may* perform quite well even if its assumptions are not satisfied. On the other hand, it is important to see that any failed assumption is a possible point of weakness in an empirical argument, to be taken seriously and anticipated if possible.

5. INTERPRETATION

Interpretation of results involving random factors differs in certain respects from interpretation involving only fixed factors. These differences follow from the different stances taken toward the *levels* of fixed and of random factors. Recall that a fixed factor is one whose specific levels are of interest, while a random factor is one whose specific levels are arbitrary and substitutable (in principle) for other arbitrary levels. Although interpretations of fixed effects often focus on each specific level of the factor, there is rarely any point in attempting to interpret random effects in this fashion. Designs with random factors (especially random factors crossed with fixed factors) require a different interpretive perspective.

To understand this point, consider a design in which the treatment variable of interest (with fixed levels) is crossed with a replication factor (with arbitrary levels), that is, a treatment × replication design (Jackson, Brashers, & Massey, 1992). In earlier chapters, we have considered two examples of treatment × replication designs: the experiment on comparative and noncomparative advertising discussed earlier as Example 3, in which arbitrary products appear crossed with ad type, and the experiment on candidate credentials discussed as Example 4, in which arbitrary sets of credentials appear crossed with candidate gender.

Treatment × replication designs have three types of effects that might be tested for significance: the treatment effects, the replication effects, and the Treatment × Replication interaction. How does interpretation of these three tests differ from interpretation of the analogous tests in a standard factorial design with only fixed factors? We note three differences.

First, in most cases, the replication main effects will be of no interest at all. In our hypothetical experiment on advertising strategy, a significant replication effect would simply indicate that for whatever reason not all products get the same response. In our hypothetical experiment on candidate gender, a significant credentials effect would simply indicate that some of the credentials are stronger than others. Notice that only in very unusual circumstances would we be interested in following up a significant F for a random factor with planned comparisons or post hoc tests, because the difference between two levels of a random factor will be a difference between two arbitrary units: a difference, for example, in purchase intentions for Flash toothpaste and Sudso detergent.

Second, the treatment effect requires subtly different interpretation. In a standard factorial with fixed factors, the main effects of each factor are considered to be parameters whose values are the same from one level to another of the other factor. In a treatment $\times$ replication design, the difference between the two treatment levels is best understood as the *average* effect of the treatment, with the treatment effect itself understood as potentially variable from one implementation to another. Recall our earlier discussion of the idea of a hypothetical average effect $\overline{\Delta}$ over all possible implementations of the treatment, each implementation having its own unique effect δ_j. This hypothetical average effect can be seen as the mean of an "effect distribution" (Hedges & Olkin, 1985; Jackson, 1991), and the average effect of the treatment within the experiment is of interest as an estimate of the mean of the effect distribution.

Consider our hypothetical experiment on advertising strategy. We are interested in whether comparative claims or noncomparative claims make for more effective ads. Quite likely the difference between the two strategies will be larger for some products than for others, and it may even be the case that a few products, for no apparent reason, favor the use of a strategy that is disadvantageous for most. We can envision each product as having its own unique treatment effect, with treatment effects varying around some average value that we would like to estimate. The test of the treatment differences in a treatment $\times$ replication design is a test of the null hypothesis that this average value is zero.

Third, the Treatment $\times$ Replication interaction figures differently in interpretation, not only in itself, but also in relation to the treatment effect. As might be anticipated from the discussion above, the Treatment $\times$ Replication interaction represents the variability of the treatment effect from one replication of the treatment to another. In fact, when the treatment has just two levels, the sum of squares for this interaction is a very simple function of the variance in the treatment differences from one level of the replication factor to another (Jackson, 1991). If the overall treatment difference is interpreted as estimating the average treatment effect, the interaction can be interpreted as estimating the variability of the effect, or the variance of the effect distribution.

Notice that this sort of stance differs markedly from the stance taken toward interactions in standard factorials with only fixed factors. A significant interaction between two fixed factors is commonly taken as grounds for *not* testing the treatment main effects but for backing the analysis down to an examination of one factor's effects at each level of the other factor. For example, if in our Example 4 we found a significant Candidate Gender × Governmental Level interaction, we would probably not be satisfied with conclusions about the overall effect of gender, but would want to know the effect of gender at each governmental level. We might want to show, for example, that the disadvantage of being female increases as the governmental level rises from local to state to federal, in which case we would want a comparison of response to male and female candidates at *each* level of government.

But this kind of examination of "simple main effects" makes far less sense when dealing with interactions between a treatment factor and a replication factor. For example, if we found a significant Gender × Credentials interaction, we would not be particularly interested in the fact that the gender difference is really pronounced for the Republican farmer running for county clerk and not as pronounced for the Democratic restaurant owner running for county recorder of deeds. Because these credentials are just arbitrary examples of backgrounds and platforms, there is no interest in the effect of gender for each one, but only in the overall or average effect of gender.

Although we will not discuss in depth the interpretation of effects in other designs with random factors, the general lesson to be taken from this brief discussion is that random factors call for a rethinking of some routinized ways of interpreting significant effects. In many texts, designs with random factors are treated entirely separately from other designs, the presumption being that the object of such designs is to estimate "variance components" that are used as measures of the variability in scores due to each factor. Of course estimation of variance components is *one* thing to do with designs with random factors, but as we have seen, there are other possibilities, especially when the random factors are not of interest in themselves, but are included to improve estimation of the effects of interest.

6. STATISTICAL POWER

As noted previously, experiments incorporating random factors require different significance tests than do standard designs involving only fixed factors. Although methods for estimation of power in fixed effects analysis are now widely familiar (most notably, Cohen, 1988), methods for estimation of power in designs with random factors are not (Koele, 1982). It should not be assumed that accurate power levels can be found by referring to tables of power levels for fixed-model tests (such as Cohen's). The adaptation of such tables to tests involving random factors requires a change in the conceptualization of effect size and a change in the unit of analysis (see Barcikowski, 1981). More important, because power to detect an effect depends not only on the size of the effect as ordinarily understood but also on the variability of the effect (e.g., from example to example or from replication to replication), the use of power analysis in designs with random factors is a very complicated and uncertain enterprise.

To evaluate the power of a test it is necessary to know the distribution of test outcomes when the null hypothesis is false. When the null hypothesis is *true,* ANOVA F tests have F distributions (or "central F distributions") determined by their numerator and denominator degrees of freedom. Knowing the null distribution allows us to evaluate the probabilities of test outcomes assuming that the null hypothesis is true; when we choose a critical value for a test we set the probability of rejecting a true null hypothesis. Recall that power is the probability of rejecting a false null hypothesis, so to evaluate power it is necessary to know how likely the test is to produce a result greater than the chosen critical value given some alternative to the null hypothesis. The nonnull distribution of F depends on the size of the experiment, the size of the effect to be tested, and (most important for the present discussion) the nature of the effect to be tested. For tests involving random factors, the nonnull distribution may be a "noncentral F distribution," or it may be a multiple of a central F distribution, or it may have some other unknown distribution (Scheffé, 1959, esp. p. 270, pp. 412-415).

Koele (1982) has provided a set of easily implemented procedures that can be applied to the evaluation of power in factorial designs. In testing fixed factors, Koele points out that F will have a noncentral F distribution when the null hypothesis is false. A noncentral F distribution is determined by its numerator and denominator degrees of freedom and by a third value, called the "noncentrality parameter," that reflects the size of the effect to be tested. This noncentrality parameter, λ, can be calculated as a function of variance components involved in the mean square for the effect to be tested. For a standard factorial with only fixed factors, Koele gives the following as the value of λ:

$$\lambda = n\Theta_T^2/\sigma_e^2$$

where

$$\Theta_T^2 = \left(\sum \tau_i^2\right)\bigg/ t$$

τ_i is the effect for the ith treatment level, σ_e^2 is the within-groups variance, n is the total number of observations, and t is the number of treatment levels. Note that Koele's $\Theta^2 = [(t - 1)/t]\theta_T^2$ as we have used θ^2 in our expressions for expected mean squares.

For factorials involving random factors crossed with the fixed factors of interest (and for other designs), the calculation of λ may be more complicated, because more error components may be involved. To generalize Koele's method, σ_e^2 is replaced by an expression representing the error term for the test. For a two-way factorial with A fixed and B random, the test for the A effects is $F = MS_A/MS_{A \times b}$, and the noncentrality parameter is thus composed as follows, with s being the number of observations per cell:

$$\lambda = n\Theta_A^2/(s\sigma_{A \times b}^2 + \sigma_e^2)$$

The power of the test for the fixed factor is the probability that the F statistic will exceed the null hypothesis critical value F_c given degrees of freedom df_{num} and df_{denom} and noncentrality parameter λ. This probability can be calculated using a simple program written in SAS, to be described in the next chapter.

For tests of the random factors, F will be a multiple κ of a central F distribution, the value of κ being a function of expected mean squares of numerator and denominator. To calculate κ, construct the appropriate F ratio to test the random factor. Then replace the numerator and denominator of the appropriate F ratio with their expected mean squares. For example, in a simple two-factor design with B random, the F ratio for testing B is $MS_b/MS_{s(Ab)}$. Replacing each MS with its corresponding expectation, we get the following:

$$\text{EMS}_b/\text{EMS}_{s(Ab)} = (as\sigma_b^2 + \sigma_{s(Ab)}^2)/\sigma_{s(Ab)}^2$$

The value of this ratio is κ, and the power of the test for the random factor is the probability that F will exceed F_c/κ, where F_c is the critical value for rejecting the null hypothesis for a test with given degrees of freedom for the numerator and denominator. This probability can also be easily calculated using SAS, as will be explained in the next chapter.

Evaluating the power of tests for interactions between fixed and random factors is more difficult. Koele recommends not bothering about calculations of power for these tests, but in many cases this test will be of interest and some general estimate of power will be important to decisions about design. In these cases, one strategy is to estimate power for interactions as for other random effects, recognizing that in some designs this may not give exact power levels. We have used simulations to check power levels calculated in this way and have found this to be a very reliable method across the design types we have examined.

For nested designs, power calculations are conducted in the same fashion as for factorial designs, changing only the calculation of λ and κ. For example, if a random factor B is nested under a fixed factor A, with individual observations nested within levels of B, the test for effects of A is $\text{MS}_A/\text{MS}_{b(A)}$ and the test for the effects of B is $\text{MS}_{b(A)}/\text{MS}_{s(Ab)}$. The power of the first test depends on the noncentrality parameter λ, which is now a function of the true differences among levels of A and the random variance contributed by both the sampled levels of B and the individual observations:

$$\lambda = n\Theta_A^2/(s\sigma_{b(A)}^2 + \sigma_{s(Ab)}^2)$$

The power of the second test depends on the multiple κ, which is calculated very simply as follows:

$$\kappa = (s\sigma_{b(A)}^2 + \sigma_{s(Ab)}^2)/\sigma_{s(Ab)}^2$$

What if there is no good way to estimate in advance the likely values of the variance components involved? This is of course a familiar general problem in power analysis, but the complexities and uncertainties are magnified by the presence of multiple random factors. Guidance in planning experiments can be found in examination of a range of plausible values considered in combination with a range of possible study sizes. A simple computer program written in SAS will be shown in the next chapter, as an example of how power analysis might be used in the planning of an experiment.

In the absence of explicit power analysis, it may be helpful to know a general principle: The larger the variance due to the random factors, the greater the number of levels needed to achieve adequate power for tests of the fixed factors (Barcikowski, 1981; Jackson & Brashers, 1990, 1992; Wickens & Keppel, 1983). Often, a plausible judgment can be made about the variability of a treatment effect based simply on the nature of the treatment implementation. Particularly vulnerable are treatments that must be embodied in complex social stimuli (such as messages or confederate behaviors) where the likelihood of incidental variations is high. When no information is available about the uniformity of such treatments' effects, our recommendation is to include as many different implementations as is practical, using the information obtained from these as a basis for planning of future experiments.

7. COMPUTER-ASSISTED ANALYSIS OF DESIGNS WITH RANDOM FACTORS

Although most researchers will use computer packages when actually analyzing their data, the previous discussion of expected mean squares and choice of test statistics remains important because many of these programs will require that the analyst provide information about which factors are fixed and which random. In some cases, appropriate analysis will depend on the researcher specifying error terms for significance tests of interest or at least verifying those chosen by the computer. And as will be discussed later, prepackaged analysis may make special or unusual assumptions that differ from what the researcher expects.

Before using any computer program to analyze designs with random factors, the analyst must have a basic familiarity with the program and its special requirements. In this chapter, we will focus on two well-known statistical packages (SAS and SPSSX), both of which are available on most university mainframe computers.[3] Some readers may prefer to read only the sections pertinent to their preferred package; others will want to compare the possibilities within these two packages.

SAS Procedures for Designs With Random Factors

Within SAS, designs with random effects can be analyzed with the GLM, NESTED, ANOVA, and VARCOMP procedures. NESTED can be used for hypothesis testing only if the factors are hierarchically nested and all factors are random. If any factors are fixed or if factors are crossed, ANOVA can be used for balanced designs and GLM for others. VARCOMP, designed specifically for estimating variance components, is useful for measurement applications (such as our Example 1, in which interest centers on the dependability of ratings from one rater to another).

The most flexible of the SAS procedures is GLM (General Linear Model). GLM requires more computer memory than NESTED or ANOVA, but is able to handle a wider variety of designs. Commands necessary to execute GLM are shown below. SAS keywords are shown in uppercase letters and our own specifications in lowercase letters; curly brackets describe the sort of specifications required at each point in a sequence.

```
PROC GLM;
     CLASS {list of factors};
     MODEL {dependent variable list} = {list of effects};
```

The CLASS statement contains a list of the classification variables (the factors). The MODEL statement indicates which effects are to be used in the analysis of the dependent variable(s). A MODEL statement contains the keyword MODEL followed by the name of a dependent variable (or list of dependent variables), followed by "=," followed by a list of effects. Interactions are written as two or more factor names linked by asterisks. In the example below, the dependent variable is Y and the design is a two-way factorial in which the main effects of A and B and the A × B interaction are to be tested.

```
     MODEL y = a b a*b;
```

For a full factorial model (all factors crossed), a simplified MODEL statement can be substituted, consisting of a list of factors separated by vertical slashes as follows:

```
     MODEL y = a|b;
```

Similarly, a full three way factorial can be written as

MODEL y = a|b|c;

instead of the more cumbersome

MODEL y = a b c a*b a*c b*c a*b*c;

If one or more factors are designated as random, the GLM procedure will generate expected mean squares and conduct mixed model analysis of variance (in addition to the default analysis treating all factors as fixed). To designate factors as random, a line is added to the program containing the keyword RANDOM, followed by the names of all effects (including interactions) that are to be considered random. In a two-factor design with one fixed factor and one random factor (such as our Example 3), the program could be written as follows:

PROC GLM;
    CLASS adtype product;
    MODEL rating = adtype product adtype*product;
    RANDOM product adtype*product/TEST;

This option should be used with great caution in factorial designs, because the program does not recognize any difference between the interaction of two random factors and the interaction of a fixed and a random factor.[4]

Greater control over the analysis can be exercised using the TEST statement to designate error terms for each hypothesis of interest. The keyword TEST is followed by keywords H and E, used to designate the hypothesis to be tested and the error term appropriate for that test, as follows:

TEST H = {effect to be tested} E = {error term};

In our example, the standard mixed model analysis could be requested using the following commands (even without a RANDOM command):

PROC GLM;
    CLASS adtype product;

```
MODEL rating = adtype product adtype*product;
TEST H = adtype E = adtype*product;
```

The TEST command above results in a test of ad type using the Ad Type × Product interaction as the error term.

Multiple TEST statements can be used if several different hypothesis tests are wanted. The TEST statement does not replace the default analysis (which is to test all effects against the within-groups or residual mean square), so no TEST statement is needed for any effect that *should* be tested using the default error term. On the other hand, the commands above will produce a printout showing two different tests for the ad type effects (one using the default error term and another using the specified error term). The fact that both tests are printed does not imply that both are useful, of course, and it is the responsibility of the user to know which to report and interpret.

Figure 7.1 shows a complete SAS program, with data, for a two-way design with one factor fixed and one random. Both RANDOM and TEST commands are illustrated, though these are entirely redundant for the example. Figure 7.2 shows the printouts that result from this program.

The GLM procedure also allows for analysis of designs with nested factors. Nesting is indicated in the MODEL statement using parentheses. In the example below, B is nested within levels of A.

```
MODEL y = a b(a);
```

If B is a random factor, the correct analysis can be obtained using either the RANDOM command or the TEST command:

```
PROC GLM;
    CLASS a b;
    MODEL y = a b(a);
    RANDOM b(a)/TEST;
```

Alternatively:

```
PROC GLM;
    CLASS a b;
    MODEL y = a b(a);
    TEST H = a E = b(a);
```

```
DATA EXAMPLE;
INPUT ID A B Y;
CARDS;

 1  1  1   11.0
 2  1  1    9.4
 3  1  1   10.3
 4  2  1    8.1
 5  2  1   10.3
 6  2  1    8.5
 7  1  2   12.6
 8  1  2   13.0
 9  1  2   13.5
10  2  2    7.9
11  2  2    8.0
12  2  2   10.1
13  1  3   10.2
14  1  3    8.5
15  1  3    6.8
16  2  3    8.0
17  2  3   10.2
18  2  3    9.7
19  1  4   13.3
20  1  4   15.9
21  1  4    9.8
22  2  4    6.1
23  2  4    7.6
24  2  4   11.1
25  1  5   10.1
26  1  5    8.6
27  1  5    9.6
28  2  5    3.8
29  2  5   10.4
30  2  5    7.5

PROC GLM;
CLASS A B;
MODEL Y = A | B;
RANDOM A A*B/TEST;
TEST H = A  E = A*B;
```

Figure 7.1. Sample Data and SAS Program for A × B Mixed Factorial Using GLM

In our Example 2, recall that individual teachers were nested within levels of the teaching method factor. Assuming that teachers are to be

The SAS System
General Linear Models Procedure
Class Level Information

Class	Levels	Values
A	2	1 2
B	5	1 2 3 4 5

Number of observations in data set = 30

Dependent Variable: Y

Source	DF	Sum of Squares	Mean Square	F Value	Pr > F
Model	9	101.063000	11.229222	3.17	0.0152
Error	20	70.926667	3.546333		
Corrected Total	29	171.989667			

R-Square	C.V.	Root MSE	Y Mean
0.587611	19.48780	1.88317	9.66333

{Results given below for fixed-effects analysis by default in SAS}

Source	DF	Type I SS	Mean Square	F Value	Pr > F
A	1	41.5363333	41.5363333	11.71	0.0027
B	4	28.2280000	7.0570000	1.99	0.1349
A*B	4	31.2986667	7.8246667	2.21	0.1050

Source	DF	Type III SS	Mean Square	F Value	Pr > F
A	1	41.5363333	41.5363333	11.71	0.0027
B	4	28.2280000	7.0570000	1.99	0.1349
A*B	4	31.2986667	7.8246667	2.21	0.1050

{Results given below for mixed-model analysis requested by RANDOM option in GLM}

Source	Type III Expected Mean Square
A	Var(Error) + 3 Var(A*B) + Q(A)
B	Var(Error) + 3 Var(A*B) + 6 Var(B)
A*B	Var(Error) + 3 Var(A*B)

Figure 7.2. SAS GLM Results for A × B Mixed Factorial

considered a random factor, the following command sequence would produce appropriate hypothesis tests:

```
PROC GLM;
    CLASS method teacher;
```

General Linear Models Procedure
Tests of Hypotheses for Mixed Model Analysis of Variance

Dependent Variable: Y
Source: A
Error: MS(A*B)

DF	Type III MS	Denominator DF	Denominator MS	F Value	Pr > F
1	41.536333333	4	7.8246666667	5.3084	0.0826

Source: B
Error: MS(A*B)

DF	Type III MS	Denominator DF	Denominator MS	F Value	Pr > F
4	7.057	4	7.8246666667	0.9019	0.5387

Source: A*B
Error: MS(Error)

DF	Type III MS	Denominator DF	Denominator MS	F Value	Pr > F
4	7.8246666667	20	3.5463333333	2.2064	0.1050

{Results given below for mixed-model analysis requested by TEST option in GLM}

Dependent Variable: Y

Tests of Hypotheses using the Type III MS for A*B as an error term

Source	DF	Type III SS	Mean Square	F Value	Pr > F
A	1	41.5363333	41.5363333	5.31	0.0826

Figure 7.2. Continued

    MODEL score = method teacher(method);
    RANDOM teacher(method)/TEST;

A SAS analysis for Example 2 using this command sequence is shown in a later section.

The nested procedure can be used for hierarchical designs of this type, if all factors are random. Nesting is indicated by the order in which factors are named in the CLASS statement. Because the design is assumed to be hierarchical, no MODEL statement is used, but the dependent variable must be named using a VAR statement as shown below:

```
PROC NESTED;
    CLASS a b;
    VAR y;
```

In the program above, B is nested within A, and two tests will be performed: a test of A using $MS_{b(a)}$ as the error term and a test of B using $MS_{w.g.}$ as the error term.

More complex designs can be specified, of course. For example, consider a design where a fixed factor A is crossed with a fixed factor B, a random factor C is nested within A and B, and subjects are nested within C. This design can be specified in GLM with the commands:

```
PROC GLM;
    CLASS a b c;
    MODEL y = a|b c(a*b);
    TEST H = a E = c(a*b);
    TEST H = b E = c(a*b);
    TEST H = a*b E = c(a*b);
```

which yields a design with the sources A, B, A × B, C(AB), and S(ABC) or within groups. Figure 7.3 gives a sample analysis of this design from SAS.

For balanced designs, SAS ANOVA can be used in place of SAS GLM, changing only the procedure name, from PROC GLM to PROC ANOVA. Like the GLM procedure, the SAS ANOVA procedure assumes that factors are fixed, but unlike GLM, ANOVA does not permit the designation of factors as random. To adapt ANOVA to designs with random factors, the TEST statement must be used.

SAS VARCOMP is tailored to studies such as our Example 1 and other applications in measurement, where the analytic aim is estimation of variance components for random factors. SAS VARCOMP generates expected mean squares and variance estimates for all effects in a design, assuming all factors *random* unless specifically designated as fixed.[5] The CLASS and MODEL statements are used as in the other analysis of variance procedures. For our example, with raters and managers crossed, we could obtain expected mean squares and estimates of variance components using the following command sequence:

The SAS System
General Linear Models Procedure
Class Level Information

Class	Levels	Values
A	2	1 2
B	2	1 2
C	10	1 2 3 4 5 6 7 8 9 10

Number of observations in data set = 30

Dependent Variable: Y

Source	DF	Sum of Squares	F Value	Pr > F
Model	9	73.09333333	2.41	0.0486
Error	20	67.36666667		
Corrected Total	29	140.46000000		

R-Square	C.V.	Y Mean
0.520385	18.17131	10.1000000

{Results given below for fixed-effects analysis by default in SAS}

Source	DF	Type I SS	F Value	Pr > F
A	1	39.90533333	11.85	0.0026
B	1	8.75605556	2.60	0.1226
A*B	1	0.16805556	0.05	0.8255
C(A*B)	6	24.26388889	1.20	0.3462

Source	DF	Type III SS	F Value	Pr > F
A	1	31.33338889	9.30	0.0063
B	1	8.75605556	2.60	0.1226
A*B	1	0.16805556	0.05	0.8255
C(A*B)	6	24.26388889	1.20	0.3462

{Results given below for mixed-model analysis requested by TEST option}

Tests of Hypotheses using the Type III MS for C(A*B) as an error term
Source	DF	Type III SS	F Value	Pr > F
A	1	31.33338889	7.75	0.0318

Tests of Hypotheses using the Type III MS for C(A*B) as an error term
Source	DF	Type III SS	F Value	Pr > F
B	1	8.75605556	2.17	0.1916

Tests of Hypotheses using the Type III MS for C(A*B) as an error term
Source	DF	Type III SS	F Value	Pr > F
A*B	1	0.16805556	0.04	0.8452

Figure 7.3. SAS GLM Results for C(AB) Design

```
PROC VARCOMP;
    CLASS rater manager;
    MODEL score = raterlmanager;
```

VARCOMP does not compute significance tests. However, because it does compute sums of squares and mean squares, any desired F test can be composed easily by hand, or the data can be passed through another ANOVA program as well to get significance tests performed.

SPSSX Procedures for Designs With Random Factors

Within SPSSX, the MANOVA procedure must be used when the design includes random factors. To execute MANOVA, variables are specified with the MANOVA command by listing the dependent variables separated from the factors by the keyword "by," as shown below. For each factor, the levels to be used in the analysis must be specified in parentheses by giving the lowest value and the highest value used to name factor levels. For example, if factor A has two levels coded 1 and 2, then A will be named in the factor list and followed by (1,2). In the example below, A has two levels and B has (at most) five.

```
MANOVA y BY a (1,2) b (1,5)
```

Without further qualifications, the command above will assume a full factorial model. Design can be specified explicitly using a DESIGN statement that simply lists the effects to be estimated and tested. Interactions are written as two or more factor names connected by the keyword BY, as in "a BY b" for the A × B interaction. The DESIGN statement appears as part of the MANOVA statement, separated from it by a slash, as shown below for a full factorial:

```
MANOVA y BY a (1,2) b (1,5)
    /DESIGN = a, b, a BY b
```

Optionally, the DESIGN statement may include specially requested hypothesis tests; because the default analysis assumes all factors fixed, the DESIGN statement is the primary mechanism offered for tailoring of the analysis to designs with random factors. Special tests are requested by associating the effect to be tested with an appropriate error mean square, using the keyword VS. Multiple error terms may be specified, but error terms other than the default (the within groups mean square, referred to as WITHIN) must be named as error terms by assigning them numeric codes from 1 to 10. For example, if in the design above B is a random factor, the DESIGN statement can be modified to name the A × B interaction as error term 1, and to specify that A is to be tested against this term, as shown below:

```
MANOVA y BY a (1,2) b (1,5)
   /DESIGN = a VS 1
      a BY b = 1 VS WITHIN
      b VS WITHIN
```

In the DESIGN statement, the first line specifies that factor A is to be tested using error term 1. The second line defines error term 1 as the A × B interaction, and further specifies that this interaction is to be tested using the within groups mean square (keyword WITHIN) as an error term. The third line specifies that factor B is to be tested against the within groups mean square. Figure 7.4 shows a complete SPSSX program, with data, for a problem of this type. SPSSX output for this design is given in Figure 7.5. Notice that this design is structured like our Example 3, the experiment on comparative and noncomparative advertising (analyzed later in the chapter using SAS). To conduct a mixed model ANOVA on this experiment using SPSSX MANOVA, we would use the following command sequence:

```
MANOVA rating BY adtype (1,2) product (1,10)
   /DESIGN = adtype VS 1
      adtype BY product = 1 VS WITHIN
      product VS WITHIN
```

Nesting is indicated by connecting two factor names with the keyword WITHIN, as in "b WITHIN a" to indicate nesting of B within levels of A. For a design with random factor B nested within fixed factor A and respondents nested within B, the following expressions generate tests of the A and B(A) factors with their appropriate error terms.

```
MANOVA y BY a (1,2), b (1,5)
   /DESIGN = a VS 1
      b WITHIN a = 1 VS WITHIN
```

```
TASK NAME              FILE: EXAMPLE1.SPS
DATA LIST             /1 ID 2-3 A 6 B 9 Y 13-16
MANOVA                Y BY A (1,2), B (1,5)
                     /DESIGN = A VS 1
                               A BY B = 1 VS WITHIN
                               B VS WITHIN
```

BEGIN DATA

```
 1  1  1   11.0
 2  1  1    9.4
 3  1  1   10.3
 4  2  1    8.1
 5  2  1   10.3
 6  2  1    8.5
 7  1  2   12.6
 8  1  2   13.0
 9  1  2   13.5
10  2  2    7.9
11  2  2    8.0
12  2  2   10.1
13  1  3   10.2
14  1  3    8.5
15  1  3    6.8
16  2  3    8.0
17  2  3   10.2
18  2  3    9.7
19  1  4   13.3
20  1  4   15.9
21  1  4    9.8
22  2  4    6.1
23  2  4    7.6
24  2  4   11.1
25  1  5   10.1
26  1  5    8.6
27  1  5    9.6
28  2  5    3.8
29  2  5   10.4
30  2  5    7.5
```

END DATA

Figure 7.4. Sample Data and SPSS Program for A × B Mixed Factorial using MANOVA

4-Jul-93 SPSSX RELEASE 4.1 FOR VAX/VMS
09:55:47 FILE: EXAMPLE1.SPS

**** A N A L Y S I S   O F   V A R I A N C E – DESIGN   1 ****

Tests of Significance for Y using UNIQUE sums of squares

Source of Variation	SS	DF	MS	F	Sig of F
WITHIN CELLS	70.93	20	3.55		
A BY B (ERROR 1)	31.30	4	7.82	2.21	.105
B	28.23	4	7.06	1.99	.135
Error 1	31.30	4	7.82		
A	41.54	1	41.54	5.31	.083

Figure 7.5. SPSS MANOVA Results for an A × B Mixed Factorial

In this DESIGN statement, the first line specifies that factor A is to be tested against error term 1, defined in the second line as the B within A mean square. B is tested using the within groups mean square as its error term.

Other Considerations: Simplified Analysis

In many cases, appropriate analysis can be simplified by redefining the unit of analysis.[6] If respondents are nested within levels of another random factor, it is often convenient to treat the levels of the other random factor as the unit of analysis, so that the respondents factor drops from view entirely and the "observations" that are actually analyzed are averages computed across individuals within levels of the other random factor.

In our discussion of Example 2, the experiment on teaching methods, the possibility of treating teacher as the unit of analysis was mentioned briefly. To implement this analytic strategy, each teacher would contribute one observation, that one observation being the average score for the teacher's class. The principal consequence of this is to transform a hierarchically nested design into a simple independent groups design (with one explanatory factor, teaching method, and observations nested within each level of method). Notice that for balanced designs, this changes neither the abstract form nor the concrete result of the test for the effect of teaching method. A side consequence of this strategy is that it gives equal weight to each teacher, even if class sizes vary from one teacher to another. Figures 7.6 and 7.7 show two versions of this problem, analyzed first with students as an explicit factor, and then with teachers as the unit of analysis, respectively. Note that the value of F for the test of the teaching method is the same in both analyses (a consequence of equal class sizes and equal numbers of teachers per method).

In Example 3, where respondents are nested within both ad type and product, a redefinition of the unit of analysis from respondents to products again simplifies the design without changing the test of the treatment effect. If each product is considered as contributing one observation (a group mean) under the comparative treatment and one observation (another group mean) under the noncomparative treatment, the treatment differences can be evaluated as though in a one-factor repeated-measures design—or for that matter, using a simple paired samples t test (Brown & Melamed, 1990). The cost of this simplification is that it is no longer possible to test the Ad Type × Product interaction, a test that might be important in fully describing the nature of the treatment effect. Figure 7.8 provides results of a computer analysis with respondent as the unit of analysis (nested within Ad Type × Product) and Figure 7.9 provides results of a computer analysis on the same data with product as the unit of analysis, using a paired-samples t test. In comparing the results, keep in mind that the F value given in Figure 7.8 should be the square of the t value given in Figure 7.9.

Computer-Assisted Power Analysis

As explained earlier, power calculations for tests involving random factors can be done quite easily within SAS. A test of a fixed factor with degrees of freedom df_1 and df_2 will have power determined by the size of the noncentrality parameter λ. This power can be calculated by SAS using the following expression:

pf = 1 − PROBF(fc,df1,df2,lambda)

where pf is simply the name we have chosen to denote the power of a test for a fixed factor, fc is the desired critical value for the test (gotten from a table of F values), df1 and df2 are the degrees of freedom for

The SAS System
General Linear Models Procedure
Class Level Information

Class	Levels	Values
TEACHER	10	1 2 3 4 5 11 12 13 14 15
METHOD	2	1 2

Number of observations in data set = 100

Dependent Variable: SCORE

Source	DF	Sum of Squares	F Value	Pr > F
Model	9	48.22523029	6.07	0.0001
Error	90	79.39297293		
Corrected Total	99	127.61820322		

R-Square	C.V.	SCORE Mean
0.377887	11.52459	8.14974940

{Results given below for fixed-effects analysis by default in SAS}

Source	DF	Type I SS	F Value	Pr > F
METHOD	1	33.13379239	37.56	0.0001
TEACHER(METHOD)	8	15.09143790	2.14	0.0400

Source	DF	Type III SS	F Value	Pr > F
METHOD	1	33.13379239	37.56	0.0001
TEACHER(METHOD)	8	15.09143790	2.14	0.0400

{Results given below for mixed-model analysis requested by RANDOM option in GLM}

Source	Type III Expected Mean Square
METHOD	Var(Error) + 10 Var(TEACHER(METHOD)) + Q(METHOD)
TEACHER(METHOD)	Var(Error) + 10 Var(TEACHER(METHOD))

Figure 7.6. Student as Unit of Analysis in Teaching Method Experiment

numerator and denominator respectively, and lambda is a stipulated value of λ. For random factors, where power depends on κ, the power can be calculated as follows:

$$pr = 1 - PROBF(fc/kappa, df1, df2)$$

General Linear Models Procedure
Tests of Hypotheses for Mixed Model Analysis of Variance

Dependent Variable: SCORE

Source: METHOD
Error: MS(TEACHER(METHOD))

DF	Type III MS	Denominator DF	Denominator MS	F Value	Pr > F
1	33.13379239	8	1.8864297377	17.5643	0.0030

Source: TEACHER(METHOD)
Error: MS(Error)

DF	Type III MS	Denominator DF	Denominator MS	F Value	Pr > F
8	1.8864297377	90	0.8821441436	2.1385	0.0400

Level of METHOD	N	----------SCORE---------- Mean	SD
1	50	7.57412980	1.00399311
2	50	8.72536900	0.95929720

{Results given below for mixed-model analysis requested by TEST option in GLM}

Dependent Variable: SCORE

Tests of Hypotheses using the Type III MS for TEACHER(METHOD) as an error term

Source	DF	Type III SS	F Value	Pr > F
METHOD	1	33.13379239	17.56	0.0030

Figure 7.6. Continued

where pr is the name used to denote the power of a test for a random factor, fc is again the critical value for the test, kappa is the stipulated value of κ, and df1 and df2 are degrees of freedom for the test of the random factor. As noted in our earlier discussion of power, this calculation may not be exact for all designs but appears reasonable as a strategy for assessing power of tests involving interaction of fixed and random factors as well as tests involving only random factors.

The SAS System
General Linear Models Procedure
Class Level Information

Class	Levels	Values
METHOD	2	1 2

Number of observations in data set = 10

Dependent Variable: SCORE

Source	DF	Sum of Squares	F Value	Pr > F
Model	1	3.31337924	17.56	0.0030
Error	8	1.50914379		
Corrected Total	9	4.82252303		

R-Square	C.V.	SCORE Mean
0.687063	5.329372	8.14974940

Source	DF	Type I SS	F Value	Pr > F
METHOD	1	3.31337924	17.56	0.0030

Source	DF	Type III SS	F Value	Pr > F
METHOD	1	3.31337924	17.56	0.0030

Level of METHOD	N	----------TEACHX---------- Mean	SD
1	5	7.57412980	0.39774648
2	5	8.72536900	0.46806376

Figure 7.7. Teacher as Unit of Analysis in Teaching Method Experiment

Power can be evaluated for varying conditions (representing different stipulated λ's or different study sizes) by repeating this calculation for some number of different values of df1, df2, and kappa or lambda as required. This would be a useful strategy for investigating the range of power values plausible for a design in which we have no prior basis for stipulating variance components, where we might simply set the variance components to a range of small, medium, and large sizes. It would also help us to determine the gain (or loss) in power to be expected from different design decisions.

For example, suppose we are planning an experiment to contrast two treatment levels, using multiple replications of the treatment contrast.

58

The SAS System
General Linear Models Procedure
Class Level Information

Class	Levels	Values
PRODUCT	10	1 2 3 4 5 6 7 8 9 10
ADTYPE	2	1 2

Number of observations in data set = 100

Dependent Variable: RATING

Source	DF	Sum of Squares	F Value	Pr > F
Model	19	112.34990832	8.01	0.0001
Error	80	59.05022852		
Corrected Total	99	171.40013684		

R-Square	C.V.	RATING Mean
0.655483	4.120173	20.8521270

Source	DF	Type I SS	F Value	Pr > F
PRODUCT	9	12.56871350	1.89	0.0649
ADTYPE	1	89.96958815	121.89	0.0001
PRODUCT*ADTYPE	9	9.81160667	1.48	0.1708

Source	DF	Type III SS	F Value	Pr > F
PRODUCT	9	12.56871350	1.89	0.0649
ADTYPE	1	89.96958815	121.89	0.0001
PRODUCT*ADTYPE	9	9.81160667	1.48	0.1708

Tests of Hypotheses using the Type III MS for PRODUCT*ADTYPE as an error term

Source	DF	Type III SS	F Value	Pr > F
ADTYPE	1	89.96958815	82.53	0.0001

Figure 7.8. Respondent as Unit of Analysis in Ad Type × Product Design

The two-leveled treatment factor is fixed, and the replication factor, with number of levels r to be determined, is considered random. The total number of observations, n, is to be divided among the $2r$ groups, and n too is to be determined. Our objective is to set r and n in such a way as to provide adequate power to detect treatment and Treatment × Replication effects. If we have no prior knowledge of the effect sizes required, we may also wish to examine a diverse range of combinations. These objectives can be pursued using a simple program like the one

Product	Ad Type 1	Ad Type 2
1	19.5022400	20.9312200
2	19.7325200	21.9474000
3	19.9425600	22.0744800
4	19.5927600	21.0002600
5	20.1417400	22.0231200
6	19.7170800	21.9571600
7	21.1994600	21.6010000
8	20.1396800	22.3428200
9	19.6874600	22.0462400
10	19.3805400	22.0828000

The SAS System

Analysis Variable : DIFF

Mean	Std Error	T	Prob > |T|
-1.8937769	0.2082953	-9.0917889	0.0001

Figure 7.9. Product as Unit of Analysis in Ad Type × Product Design

shown in Figure 7.10. The program does an analysis, for each combination of treatment and Treatment × Replication variance components, of the power that results from dividing a fixed pool of respondents among 5, 10, or 20 independent replications. A portion of the output from the program is shown in Table 7.1.

Notice in Table 7.1 that, given a set number of respondents (400), the power of the test of the treatment effects increases with an increase in the levels of the replication factor, while the power of the interaction test decreases with an increase in the levels of this factor. Note too that the power to detect treatment effects declines with an increase in the size of the Treatment × Replication variance component, a point mentioned earlier and illustrated concretely here.

Although SPSSX MANOVA does calculate power levels for some tests, the limitations within this program rule out its use for the sort of problems considered here.

60

Program and Data	Explanation
data power;	{names dataset}
input n t r fc1 fc2;	{input variables
	n = number of observations
	t = treatment levels
	r = replication levels
	fc1 = critical value for test 1
	fc2 = critical value for test 2}
df1 = t - 1;	
df2 = (r - 1);	{degrees of freedom}
df3 = n - t*r;	
s = n/(t*r);	{s = number of observations per cell}
do thetasq = .01, .04;	{thetasq = standardized θ^2_T}
do sigmasq = .025, .05;	{sigmasq = standardized $\sigma^2_{T \times r}$}
	{specifying multiple values for the two variance components allows examination of how power depends on effect size}
lambda = n*thetasq/(s*sigmasq + 1);	{noncentrality parameter for test 1}
kappa = 1 + s*sigmasq;	{multiple for test 2}
	{lambda and kappa must be adapted to the design and to the tests desired}
pf = 1 - probf(fc1,df1,df2,lambda);	{computes power for treatment test}
pr = 1 - probf(fc2/kappa,df2,df3);	{computes power for interaction test}
output;	
end;	
end;	
cards;	
200 2 5 7.7086 2.4192	
200 2 10 5.1174 1.9322	
200 2 20 4.3808 1.6519	{design sizes of interest, together with appropriate
400 2 5 7.7086 2.3948	critical values gotten from tables or other source}
400 2 10 5.1174 1.9045	
400 2 20 4.3808 1.6155	
;	
proc tabulate;	{generates tabulation of power values for varying
class n r thetasq sigmasq;	study sizes and effect sizes}
var pf pr;	
table (thetasq*sigmasq), (n*r),	
(pf pr)*mean/condense;	

Figure 7.10. SAS Program for Evaluating Power in Treatment × Replication Design

Table 7.1
Power to Detect Treatment Effect and Treatment × Replication
Interaction (two treatment levels, r replications), with $\theta_T^2 = .04$

$\sigma^2_{T \times r}$	n	r	Treatment	Interaction
.025	200	5	.42	.17
		10	.62	.14
		20	.72	.10
	400	5	.57	.31
		10	.83	.25
		20	.92	.18
.05	200	5	.34	.31
		10	.54	.25
		20	.67	.18
	400	5	.42	.53
		10	.71	.48
		20	.87	.37

8. CONCLUSION

At present, analytic methods involving factors treated as random are not widely used. This does not mean that they are not widely useful. In many cases, factors that should be treated as random have been treated as fixed, to the detriment of the conclusions' validity.

Treating a factor as random rather than as fixed involves not only a substantial increase in conceptual difficulty, but also a good deal of extra work. Random factors require more attention by the researcher, and more direct responsibility for the correctness of the analysis. Planning a design with random factors inevitably means paying attention to whether the design will support tests of the effects of interest, and whether these tests will involve special difficulties such as the need to construct quasi F ratios. Because routine practice is to treat most factors as fixed, many common computer programs assume fixed effects, and the adaptation of these programs to designs with random factors is effortful. Methods for calculating power are less available for designs with random factors than for designs with fixed factors. Even interpretation of results is complicated by the decision to treat factors as random.

But weighed against this increased burden on the researcher is the increased credibility we can attach to conclusions drawn about social processes when sampled factors are treated as random. When a conclusion about the effect of a treatment is supported by a test in which examples of the treatment contrast or replications of the treatment implementation are treated as fixed, a reasonable skeptic can grant that *these arbitrary cases* yield the effect claimed, but challenge the scientific worth of the conclusion on two quite different grounds. First, the interest value of the conclusion can be challenged on the grounds that it has been shown to hold only for some small set of arbitrary cases, cases that in themselves are of no particular interest. This would generally be understood as a challenge to the external validity of the research. Second, more subtly, the conclusion can be challenged on the grounds that it depends on an arbitrary interpretation of the differences among a set of concrete cases that, among other things, vary in the factor of interest. Recall the example of the 10 confederates, and the idea that each confederate brings to the contrasting roles required not only an enactment of the treatment variable but also incidental performance features. An analysis in which confederates are treated as fixed allows these incidental features to be counted as definitive of the treatment effect, even if they have nothing to do with the treatment as conceptualized and as described theoretically. Challenges along these lines, invited by treatment of examples and replications as fixed, would ordinarily be understood as issues of internal validity.

A conclusion supported by an analysis in which examples or replications are treated as random is not vulnerable to these or similar challenges, because such an analysis takes into account the variability of the effect from case to case. Although generalization is obviously a central motivation for treating sampled levels as random, this is by no means the only way in which random factors can contribute to the strength of conclusions. Equally important is the contribution of random factors to the interpretability of the results. Designs in which treatments are replicated in multiple sets of materials, for example, improve on internal validity, by avoiding a confounding of the contrast of interest with arbitrary features of a treatment implementation and by organizing the analysis to focus on the theoretical variable rather than on its concrete implementation. Although not every experiment in social and behavioral research will require incorporation of random factors, the opportunities for strengthening both internal and external validity in this way are numerous.

NOTES

1. In a one-factor independent groups design, $\sigma^2_{s(T)}$ is a residual term containing error and other unanalyzed sources of variance. Our use of $\sigma^2_{s(T)}$ where σ^2_ε might otherwise be used is a harmless device that simplifies the application of this algorithm; in every imaginable design, error in an abstract sense is confounded with something that can be considered a factor, such as subjects, and we choose to highlight the factor as the source of randomness for reasons that will shortly become clear.

2. Clark's inclusion of σ^2_ε terms is conventional, the point being to distinguish conceptually between the Respondent × Word interaction and error that cannot be given any substantive interpretation. Within this design, the two sources of variance are indistinguishable, as is obvious from the fact that they appear everywhere linked with one another.

3. SAS, GLM, ANOVA, NESTED, and VARCOMP are registered trade names of products of SAS Institute, Inc. A general introduction to SAS is available in Spector (1993). SPSSX and MANOVA are registered trade names of products of SPSS Inc. Users' guides for all programs are regularly updated and widely available.

4. In technical terms, SAS GLM ignores a certain constraint ordinarily assumed to hold for interactions between fixed and random factors: that for any one level of the random factor, the interaction terms sum to zero across levels of the fixed factor. This has no consequence for tests of fixed factors or for tests of interactions between fixed and random factors, but it does have consequences for tests of random factors.

5. As with SAS GLM, use of SAS VARCOMP to generate expected mean squares for mixed factorials may have unexpected results, for reasons mentioned in Note 4. Possible problems occur for expected mean squares of random factors if crossed with any fixed factors, because there is no way to force a sum-to-zero constraint commonly associated with mixed model applications in the social sciences.

6. Thanks to David Kenny for pointing out this possibility.

REFERENCES

BARCIKOWSKI, R. S. (1981) "Statistical power with group mean as the unit of analysis." *Journal of Educational Statistics* 6: 267-285.

BROWN, S. R., and MELAMED, L. E. (1990) *Experimental Design and Analysis.* Sage University Paper series on Quantitative Applications in the Social Sciences, 07-074. Newbury Park, CA: Sage.

CLARK, H. H. (1973) "The language-as-fixed-effect fallacy." *Journal of Verbal Learning and Verbal Behavior* 12: 335-359.

COHEN, J. (1988) *Statistical Power Analysis (2nd ed.).* Hillsdale, NJ: Lawrence Erlbaum.

COLEMAN, E. B. (1964) "Generalizing to a language population." *Psychological Reports* 14: 219-226.

CORNFIELD, J., and TUKEY, J. W. (1956) "Average values of mean squares for factorials." *Annals of Mathematical Statistics* 27: 907-948.

CRONBACH, L. J., GLESER, G. C., NANDA, H., and RAJARATNAM, N. (1972) *The Dependability of Behavioral Measurements.* New York: John Wiley.

FONTANELLE, G. A., PHILLIPS, A. P., and LANE, D. M. (1985) "Generalizing across stimuli as well as subjects: A neglected aspect of external validity." *Journal of Applied Psychology* 70: 101-107.

FORSTER, K. I., and DICKINSON, R. G. (1976) "More on the language-as-fixed-effect fallacy: Monte Carlo estimates of error rates for F1, F2, F', and min F'." *Journal of Verbal Learning and Verbal Behavior* 15: 132-142.

GLASS, G. V., and STANLEY, J. C. (1970) *Statistical Methods in Education and Psychology.* Englewood Cliffs, NJ: Prentice Hall.

GIRDEN, E. R. (1992) *ANOVA: Repeated Measures.* Sage University Paper series on Quantitative Applications in the Social Sciences, 07-084. Newbury Park, CA: Sage.

GREENHOUSE, S. W., & GEISSER, S. (1959) "On methods in the analysis of profile data." *Psychometrika* 24(2): 95-112.

HAYS, W. L. (1981) *Statistics (3rd ed.).* New York: Holt, Rinehart & Winston.

HEDGES, L. V., and OLKIN, I. (1985) *Statistical Methods for Meta-Analysis.* San Diego, CA: Academic Press.

HOPKINS, K. D. (1984) "Generalizability theory and experimental design: Incongruity between analysis and inference." *American Educational Research Journal* 21: 703-712.

IVERSON, G. R., and NORPOTH, H. (1987) *Analysis of Variance (2nd ed.).* Sage University Paper series on Quantitative Applications in the Social Sciences, 07-001. Newbury Park, CA: Sage.

JACKSON, S. (1991) "Meta-analysis for primary and secondary data analysis: The super-experiment metaphor." *Communication Monographs* 58: 449-462.

JACKSON, S. (1992) *Message Effects Research: Principles of Design and Analysis.* New York: Guilford.

JACKSON, S., and BRASHERS, D. (1990, June) "M = ? (Choosing a 'message sample' size in communication experiments)." Paper presented at International Communication Association Meetings, Dublin.

JACKSON, S., and BRASHERS, D. E. (1992, May) "Testing treatment effects in replicated treatments designs: An empirical comparison of two candidate tests." Paper presented at International Communication Association Meetings, Miami.

JACKSON, S., and BRASHERS, D. E. (1993, May) "Assuming independence when dependence is not evident: A fallacy of misplaced presumption." Paper presented at International Communication Association Meetings, Washington, D.C.

JACKSON, S., BRASHERS, D. E., and MASSEY, J. (1992) "Statistical testing in treatment by replication designs: Three options reconsidered." *Communication Quarterly* 40: 211-227.

JACKSON, S., and JACOBS, S. (1983) "Generalizing about messages: Suggestions for the design and analysis of experiments." *Human Communication Research* 9: 169-191.

KENNY, D. A., and JUDD, C. M. (1986) "Consequences of violating the independence assumption in analysis of variance." *Psychological Bulletin* 99: 422-431.

KEPPEL, G. (1982) *Design and Analysis: A Researcher's Handbook (2nd ed.)*. Englewood Cliffs, NJ: Prentice Hall.

KEPPEL, G. (1991) *Design and Analysis: A Researcher's Handbook (3rd ed.)*. Englewood Cliffs, NJ: Prentice Hall.

KOELE, P. (1982) "Calculating power in analysis of variance." *Psychological Bulletin* 92: 513-516.

MALGADY, R. G., AMATO, J. A., and HUCK, S. W. (1979) "The fixed-effect fallacy in educational research: A problem of generalizing to multiple populations." *Educational Psychologist* 14: 79-86.

MAXWELL, S. F., and BRAY, J. H. (1986) "Robustness of the quasi F statistic to violations of sphericity." *Psychological Bulletin* 99: 416-421.

RICHTER, M. L., and SEAY, M. B. (1987) "ANOVA designs with subjects and stimuli as random effects: Applications to prototype effects on recognition memory." *Journal of Personality and Social Psychology* 53: 470-480.

SANTA, J. L., MILLER, J. J., and SHAW, M. L. (1979) "Using quasi F to prevent alpha inflation due to stimulus variation." *Psychological Bulletin* 86: 37-46.

SATTERTHWAITE, F. E. (1946) "An approximate distribution of estimates of variance components." *Biometrics Bulletin* 2: 110-114.

SCHEFFÉ, H. (1959) *The Analysis of Variance*. New York: John Wiley.

SHAVELSON, R. J., and WEBB, N. M. (1991) *Generalizability Theory: A Primer*. Newbury Park, CA: Sage.

SPECTOR, P. E. (1981) *Research Designs*. Sage University Paper series on Quantitative Applications in the Social Sciences, 07-023. Beverly Hills, CA: Sage.

SPECTOR, P. E. (1993) *SAS Programming for Researchers and Social Scientists*. Newbury Park, CA: Sage.

VAUGHAN, G. M., and CORBALLIS, M. C. (1969) "Beyond tests of significance: Estimating strength of effects in selected ANOVA designs." *Psychological Bulletin* 72: 204-213.

WICKENS, T. D., and KEPPEL, G. (1983) "On the choice of design and of test statistic in the analysis of experiments with sampled materials." *Journal of Verbal Learning and Verbal Behavior* 22: 296-309.

WIKE, E. L., and CHURCH, J. D. (1976) "Comments on Clark's 'The Language-as-Fixed-Effect Fallacy.' " *Journal of Verbal Learning and Verbal Behavior* 15: 249-255.

WINER, B. J. (1971) *Statistical Principles in Experimental Design (2nd ed.)*. New York: McGraw-Hill.

ABOUT THE AUTHORS

SALLY JACKSON is Associate Professor of Communication at the University of Arizona. She is author of *Message Effects Research: Principles of Design and Analysis* and coauthor of *Reconstructing Argumentative Discourse.* She presently serves as Associate Editor of *Human Communication Research* and as an editorial board member for several other communication research journals. Her principal methodological interests are in problems of generalization.

DALE E. BRASHERS is Assistant Professor of Communication at the Ohio State University. His substantive interest in group influence processes gives rise to methodological interest in unit of analysis and replication. He has published articles on these topics in *Communication Monographs, Communication Studies, Communication Quarterly, The Southern Journal of Communication,* and *Western States Communication Journal.*

Quantitative Applications in the Social Sciences

A SAGE UNIVERSITY PAPERS SERIES

$9.50 each

SAGE PUBLICATIONS, INC.
P.O. BOX 5084
THOUSAND OAKS, CALIFORNIA 91359-9924